# Peoples and Cultures of Uganda

Compiled by
Richard Nzita & Mbaga Niwampa

**Fountain Publishers**

Fountain Publishers Ltd.
P.O. Box 488
Kampala

© Fountain Publishers 1993
First published 1993
Second edition 1995
Third edition 1997
Reprinted 1998

ISBN 9970 02 0315

# Contents

# Acknowledgements

The publishers are grateful to various individuals and institutions for their assistance in compiling and illustrating this book.

Special mention goes to Mr. Ephraim Kamuhangire of the Department of Antiquities and Dr. Joshua Muvumba for their critical comments on the manuscript. We are also grateful to Mr. Adolu Otojoka of Makerere University, Department of Music, Dance and Drama (MDD) for his contribution on musical instruments; and to Mr. Bruno Serunkuma of the School of Fine Art, Makerere University for his contribution on Traditional Crafts.

We are equally grateful to Mr. James Sebaduka and Mr. Ezra Musiime of Uganda Museum for most of the photographs used in this book.

# Publisher's Note

The ethnic boundaries shown on all maps in this book are approximate and do not have any political or administrative connotations.

We also wish to note that this book does not cover all the recognized ethnic groups. Those on which there was insufficient information were covered under the nearest ethnic groups.

# Preface

There is no one Ugandan culture. In fact, there are as many cultures as there are peoples. There are diverse cultural groups speaking more than thirty-three languages. We have the Bantu communities, the Luo, Sudanic speaking and the Atekerin.

Culture, like a person is born, grows and dies. The cultures of different peoples in Uganda were moulded by both the natural and social environments obtaining in the specific areas where a particular people lived or migrated from.

Culture which identifies and distinguishes one society from another is a result of man's interaction with his environment, for example, those who lived in forest areas developed a different culture from those in savanna areas. Those who lived in dry areas took up different occupations which in turn shaped their way of life differently from those in wet regions. People who lived in mountainous regions behaved differently from those in valleys or plains.

The Bagisu, Bakiga and Bakonjo did not develop a monarchical system of government partly because of the mountainous terrain they had in common. The lake-shore peoples around Lakes Victoria, Kioga and Albert tended to evolve a similar culture.

## Definition of culture

There is no precise definition of culture but we can say that culture is the total sum of a people's way of life. This includes norms and values of a society; their religion, politics, economics, technology, medicine, marriage rules, songs and dances, law, eating habits, artifacts, etc.

Some people have taken culture to mean traditional dances, songs, social rituals and artifacts only. Although these constitute part of culture they are by no means the only ones. People's political behaviour and system also constitute their political culture, how it is produced and distributed among the members of that society, constitutes their economic culture.

Culture, as we pointed out earlier, is born and grows. It is a natural phenomenon. It evolves in the course of a particular society's development. It is never static. It is dynamic. We can talk of traditional as well as modern culture. A society normally adjusts its way of living in order to cope with a new and changing environment. Culture also changes due to advancement in knowledge and skills. Some aspects of culture are acquired in the course of interaction with people of faraway regions and cultures. If a society fails to adapt to a changing environment, it is bound to stagnate.

The cultures of people which have been moulded over many centuries cannot die away very easily. People have a nostalgia for the past, actual or imagined. They feel or miss the presumed good old days. The people will always want to cling to what used to identify them; sometimes even when it is counterproductive in the advancement of that society.

Culture plays very significant roles in society. People always want to have an identity. This identity is achieved through evolving specific ways of living, different from other societies.

People, unlike animals, consciously live in communities. They do not come and stay together merely because of their natural instincts. They also have a creative capacity by which they constantly improve on their well-being.

As people live in large communities they are likely to come into conflict. As such they need rules to govern their social relationships. If these rules were not there, there would be total anarchy. To avoid chaos, people, as socially creative and conscious beings, evolved norms of social living. They specified what one is expected to do and not to do. They came up with the standard behaviour expected of an individual and society and prescribed punishments (sanctions) for those who deviated from the norms of that particular society. All these norms constituted a social environment that enabled people's culture. These cultural achievements help man to tame nature and exploit it for his well-being. The technical skills enable man to shape tools that he uses to satisfy his material and spiritual needs. Tools like hoes enabled man to cultivate and get more food. Other tools like musical instruments help man to satisfy his artistic needs. These tools make up the material culture of the people.

As people live in large communities commonly called nations, they need systems to regulate their behaviour. They require public authority. This gives rise to a political culture and is a necessary aspect of social existence.

The culture of a society guides its day-to-day activities. If, for example, a society lacks a culture to govern and guide it to right attitudes to work, it is bound to have a lot of idle people. If it does not evolve social rules to discourage extramarital sex, for example, it is likely to have marital instabilities. These cultural rules and obligations need not be written.

It is said and believed that a society without culture is bound to lose its identity and be swallowed up by other cultures. Therefore, a society always jealously guards against adopting new ways of living for fear of losing its identity. This is an unnecessary fear. A society does not have to stick to its past or present culture. It can always learn and adopt new traits thus acquire a new identity. For example, a certain nationality can allow its identity to fade away in favour of a national culture.

### Transmission of culture

Culture is transmitted in many different ways. The most important medium of transmission is language. Language in Uganda distinguishes one cultural society from another. Through oral communication, culture is transmitted from generation to generation. This was more so in pre-colonial days when the art of writing was absent.

In pre-colonial Uganda, young ones were taught culture by their parents and other elders and by their peer groups with whom they interacted. They were also learning on the job. As an individual interacted with his immediate environment, both social and natural, he learnt the culture of his people.

### Interpretations of African culture

When Europeans appeared on the scene at the turn of the last century, they came face to face with new cultures. Their initial reaction was a biased one. They judged the African cultures from the point of view of European civilisation. Hence it was presumed that Ugandan Africans had no culture and civilisation. As such, the Europeans who came here embarked on a "civilising" mission.

European authors who were the first to write on the cultures and peoples of Uganda described them as primitive. These writers and missionaries wanted to "save" Africans from their cultures. One way of achieving this was to teach Africans that their ways of living were not civilised.

Africans' ways of living were described in derogatory terms. This European way of looking at African cultures had elements of racism. Physical features of Ugandans were described in a negative manner. Such descriptions as Africans "have ugly faces," "big and thick lips" and "are as agile as monkeys in climbing trees," were common. These descriptions are found in many books written by Europeans on Ugandan Africans during the first half of the 20th century.

This Eurocentric way of looking at Africans as primitive peoples is better reflected in the way Africans were described as "tribes." The standard book for British anthropologists written in 1951 describes a tribe as " a political or socially coherent and autonomous group occupying or claiming a particular territory."

According to the above definition, the Belgians or French or Russians would qualify as much as Baganda or Batooro to be called a tribe. However, the latter were and are not referred to as tribes. According to the European standard way of looking at a tribe, it is that community of barbaric peoples who are still at a very early stage of human development.

Today when different tribes in the former Yugoslavia or Russia fight each other, they call it "nationality clashes," but when it is different tribes in Uganda or Kenya it is "tribal clashes." This is due to racism. In fact some so-called tribes in Uganda such as the Banyankore or the Baganda are bigger than some nations and nationalities in Europe.

Ugandans have perhaps experienced the greatest changes in their cultures in this century alone. This is on account of, among other factors, modern technology introduced from Europe and is due to modern communication and interactions with many peoples from different continents.

But perhaps the most important factor was western education. Through this education coupled with Christian missionary evangelism, Africans were taught to despise their cultures. They were encouraged to admire European cultures an d adopt them. In the past and to some extent the present, some Africans felt that European cultures were superior to others. As such, Africans abandoned theirs in favour of European ones.

In this book, the authors maintain that Ugandans, just like any other people, had their cultures before the colonialists came. These cultures were evolving idependently, adopting some aspects from other Uganda ethnic cultures and have also acquired some from European cultures. However, there are elements of pre-colonial cultures still practised among the different Ugandan societies. The authors have tried to describe these different aspects of traditional cultures in this book.

The authors have not attempted to depict the superiority or inferiority of the different cultures. They have only given a variety of the rich cultural heritage of Uganda, a melting pot of African cultures.

**Mwambutsya-Ndebesa**
**Lecturer, History Dept.**
**Makerere University, Kampala**

# Uganda Districts

# The Settlement and Classification of the Peoples of Uganda

## Geographical background

Uganda lies entirely between the two arms of the great rift valley in East Africa. To the west, Uganda borders Zaire (former Belgian Congo). This border coincides with the western Rift Valley occupied from north to south by Lakes Albert, Edward, George and Kivu. On this border with Zaire exist also, the Rwenzori mountain ranges, the highest point of which (Mt. Margherita) is 5,119 metres high. Further south-west between Lake Edward and Lake Kivu, there is the volcanic Muhabura range protruding from the Rift Valley between 3,500 metres and 4,000 metres high.

In the north, Uganda borders the Sudan. The final demarcation of this boarder was fixed in 1914 giving the Lado enclave to the Sudan and transferring West Nile from Belgian Congo to Uganda. To the east, Uganda borders Kenya. Before 1902 the eastern boundary had extended as far as Lake Turkana. Gradual adjustments by the British who were ruling both Uganda and Kenya (then British East Africa) finally fixed the eastern boundary of Uganda in its present position in 1926.

To the south, Uganda borders Tanzania (former German East Africa). Boundary adjustments in 1910 between the British, the Belgians and the Germans fixed the southern limit of Uganda by including in Uganda, Kigezi which was formerly part of Belgian Congo and Bufumbira, formerly part of German East Africa. Kigezi was formely part of Rwanda which together with Burundi and Tanganyika, formed German East Africa.

Generally, Uganda is a land of plateaus though in some areas there are hills which are 200 metres to 500 metres high. In most places the hills are heavily eroded. In the extreme west, the ancient tabular areas still remain.

The Equator crosses southern Uganda and the climate is equatorial but moderated by altitude. On the northern shores of Lake Victoria, it rains almost throughout the year. In the rest of the country, a dry season or two occur in a year. The highest temperatures occur on the Lake Albert flats while the lowest temperatures occur on the glaciated zone of Mt. Rwenzori.

Much of southern Uganda was formerly covered by equatorial forests but most of these have now been cleared for human settlement. This has occurred particularly around Lake Victoria but some forests still exist on the Sese Islands and in the swampy zones between Lake Victoria, Lake Kioga, Lake Albert and to the south of Lake Edward along the border with Zaire. In the higher regions, the vegetation groups itself in levels such that thick forest with undergrowth of liana appear at the bottom on the lower slopes. Mountain forest extends to about 3,200 metres and above this, there are bamboo groves and alpine prairie.

## The settlement of Uganda

The present country of Uganda was forged by the British between 1890 and 1926. The name of Uganda was derived from the ancient kingdom of Buganda.

The earliest inhabitants of Uganda were the Stone-Age people. These people were gradually absorbed or replaced in the first millennium A.D. by the incoming agriculturalists and pastoralists. At the time of the coming of the British, there were over thirty ethnic groups in Uganda. These ethnic communities could conveniently be divided into four broad linguistic categories namely: the Bantu, the Luo, the Atekerin and the Sudanic.

The Bantu occupy the southern half of the country and, taken together, they constitute over 50 percent of Uganda's total population. They were the earliest group to come to Uganda and they comprise: the Baganda, the Banyoro, the Basoga, the Bagisu, the Banyankore, the Bakiga, the Bafumbira, the Batooro, the Bakonjo, the Bamba, the Batwa, the Banyole, the Basamia-Bagwe and the Bagwere. Generally they occupy the east, central, west and southern Uganda.

The second category is the Atekerin group. This group is variously referred to as the Para-Nilotics, the Lango or the Nilo-Hamites. These are found in the north, the east and north-eastern Uganda. The group constitutes the Langi, the Karimojong, the Iteso, the Kakwa and the Kumam. They trace their origins to Ethiopia and are said to have been one people. Through migrations, they came to settle in different parts of Uganda and they have developed particular characteristics which tend to distinguish them from one another. For instance, the Langi lost their Ateker language and spoke Lwo.

The final category is the Luo group. These trace their origin from southern Sudan. They are found in West Nile, northern and eastern Uganda. They constitute: the Acholi, the Alur, the Jonam and the Jopadhola. Basamia claim connection with the Luo of Kenya but they are basically Bantu.

The final category is the Sudanic speakers of West Nile. This group comprises the Madi, the Lugbara, the Okebu, the Bari, and the Metu. They trace their origin to the Sudan but their cultures and language indicate that they have become completely detached from their places of origin. With the coming of colonialism, the Lugbara tended to dominate other groups as the Lugbara language was encouraged in all primary schools as a medium of instruction.

At present, it is difficult to demarcate the confines of any one of the ethnicities described above. Colonialism, education, monetisation, easy transport and urbanisation have led to the break up or at least the loosening of cultural ties thereby leading to intermarriages and intermixtures which make it difficult to categorise, let alone demarcate the confines of different ethnicities of Uganda. However, cultural ties still bind people and though intermixing has happened on a large scale since colonialism, intermarriage is not very common and people still prefer to identify themselves by their different ethnic backgrounds. This has been the cornerstone of tribalism in post-colonial Uganda.

## The earliest man-creature

The direct ancestor of modern man is said to have been *Homo habilis*. This creature is said to have had the knowledge of making and using tools. He is thought to have been contemporaneous with *Australopithecines*, the first creature to walk on two legs. Traces of these most ancient human creatures in Uganda were found at Rusinga and Moroto. The type of creature identified at these sites was *Dryopithecus*. It was a partially bipedal creature said to have existed as far back as between thirty and fifteen million years ago.

## Stone-Age man

The earliest man in Uganda lived around 60,000–50,000 B.C. This was the early Stone Age man known as *Homo erectus*.

Traces of *Homo erectus* in Uganda

*Uganda ethnic groups*

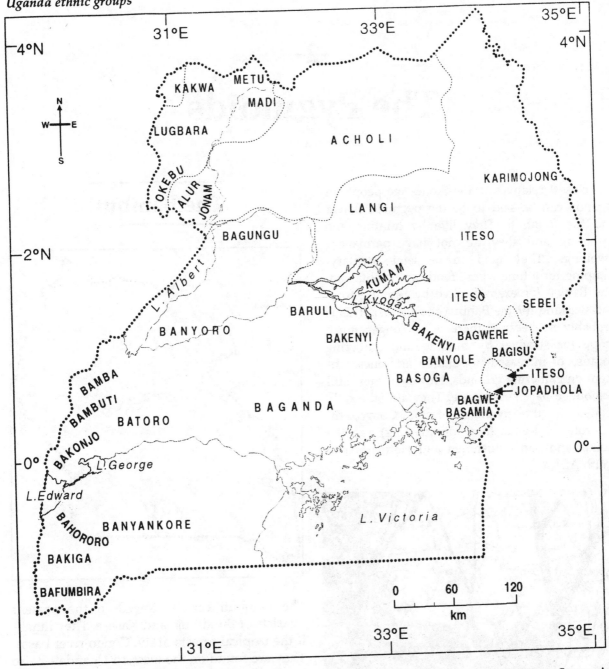

were found at Nsongezi. He had the knowledge of making and using stone tools, especially the hand-axe. Between 50,000 and 150,000 B.C., there emerged the Middle Stone-Age man. During this period, man invented fire and more stone tools and began to become widely distributed. In Uganda, sites of the Middle Stone-Age man can be traced at Nsongezi and Sango Bay.

The development of the present man is said to have taken place during the period 10,000 to 1,500 B.C. This falls within the Late Stone-Age period which is said to have lasted between some five hundred to six hundred years but traces of which still exist in most African societies. Between A.D. 500 and 1,500, other peoples began to migrate to Uganda from different parts of Africa. The first and largest group of such people was the Bantu. The earliest surviving inhabitants the Bantu found in Uganda are the pygmaean Batwa and the Bambuti.

# -2-

# The Pygmoids

The closest relatives to the Stone-Age people in Uganda can be said to be the pygmoid Batwa and the Bambuti. They live by hunting and gathering and they do not have permanent dwellings. They tend to be semi-sedentary, camping for a time where food can be obtained. The Batwa, for example, live by begging from and working for the Bahutu and Batutsi. This is probably so because there is no longer much scope for survival by hunting and gathering because of increased population and encroachment on gathering grounds. However, they still eke out a bare subsistence. They are ethnically related to the pygmies of the Congo, the Ndorobo of Kenya (now diminishing) and the Koikoi and San (Bushmen and Hottentots) of South Africa.

## The Bambuti

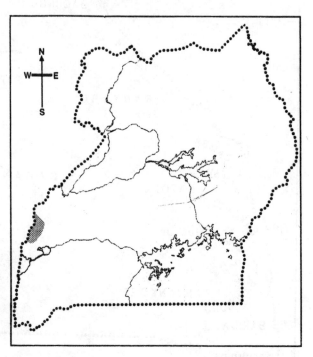

*Ndorobo men placing a beehive in a tree*

The Bambuti can be traced in the present districts of Bundibujo and Kasese. They inhabit the tropical forests of the Congo river basin. They are found on the western Uganda - Zaire border particularly in the parts adjoining the Ituri forest near the Ituri river which has its source in the Bulega hills overlooking Lake Albert and River Semuliki. The Bambuti are often referred to as pygmies and they are believed to have been the original inhabitants of the Rwenzori Mountain areas before the arrival of the Bantu. Their original home is said to have been the Congo forest. Their language is called *Kumbuti*. It is said to be very complex and difficult to learn.

## Dwellings

The Bambuti are nomads always on the move from place to place, hunting and gathering. They are said to be cannibals and their average height is about 1.5 metres. They have a light bronze colour and a beautiful complexion. They have the same curly, woolly hair as their Bantu neighbours. Their faces are broad, their nostrils wide and their lips are extraordinarily thick.

Their huts are built on the same model as Bantu huts but are made of leaves, not grass. They are round, very short, and with a small entrance so small and low that they crawl on their hands and knees when entering and getting out. Their huts are temporary due to their nomadic lifestyle.

## Food

Their diet is basically composed of meat. Often, they supplement it with bananas and sweet potatoes which they obtain by bartering meat for them with their Bantu neighbours. Sometimes they do not wait to barter. They can simply invade one's shamba and gather the produce without seeking the permission of the owner. Their neighbours fear them because of their aggressiveness. The sight of a Mwambuti (singular of Bambuti) in one's shamba may lead to the family of the owner going into temporary hiding.

They obtain their food by hunting and they are very skilled at it. When in the forest hunting, a dozen of them will make less noise than that of the animal being tracked. They arm themselves with the weapons best suited for their prey. Their normal weapons are spears, bows and arrows. Every Mwambuti is armed with a small bow; barbed, poisoned arrows; and a spear with a blade similar to those of the Batwa. When hunting, they stealthily wait by water pools and tracks used by the game. If they kill big game like an elephant, the whole colony of them, often as many as one hundred, will build their huts around the carcass of the elephant and eat it until it is finished. It is said that a fully grown elephant can feed a colony of the Bambuti for a week or more.

## Dressing

Their dress is composed of a belt wound round the waist, with a piece of barkcloth attached to the belt in the middle of the back, brought down between the legs and fixed against the belt in front. This type of dress suits both men and women but it is not very common for the Bambuti to put on clothes. They usually go stark naked though, occasionally, some of them may be found with a brass-wire bangle.

## Economy

The Bambuti's economy is just as simple as their general way of life. They are wanderers by nature with no fixed place of abode. Their chief means of subsistence is meat and the forests where they live abound with elephants, monkeys, lizards and some antelopes. The Bambuti prey on these animals and several others which the forest contains.

As one would expect, the Bambuti have no home industries. Their mode of life is purely subsistence and they do not seem to be troubled by lack of home comfort. If the Mwambuti can find somewhere to sit and a skin to sleep on, if he has eaten and drunk he finds nothing to trouble the world for.

Their other utensils besides skins include: earthenware pots (traded or stolen) and weapons. Besides these named utensils , there is no other evidence of what one would call "wealth" among the Bambuti. They seem to be contented with what they have and if it was not for the continuous heavy rains in their country, they may even have dispensed with the hut.

## Movements

When on their normal travels, the women carry all the family property. They also do all the work including the construction of huts. The man only carries his spears and arrows. The men do the hunting and really excel at it.

-3-

# The Bantu

The Bantu are a group of people who speak related languages and have similar social characteristics. They occupy a large part of Zaire and southern as well as eastern Africa. The Bantu are said to have originated from somewhere in the Congo region of central Africa and spread rapidly to southern and eastern Africa. (Today, more than one half of the population of Uganda are Bantu.) There are several groups speaking different Bantu languages.

Bantu are said to have settled in Uganda between A.D 1000 and A.D. 1300. Some reasons are given to explain why the Bantu moved from their original homeland to come to settle in Uganda. One reason is that they might have been overpopulated and therefore some groups decided to move away in search of vacant lands on which to practice agriculture. Another reason given is that they might have moved away just in search of fertile lands or due to internal conflicts within their communities or external attacks by their neighbours. Other reasons suggested include diseases and other natural disasters which might have made them uncomfortable in their homeland and so they decided to move away. One other reason is that they might have been encouraged to move away in quest of adventure and this was because they had invented iron tools which enabled them to confront wild animals and other obstacles during their movements.

Having moved away from their original homeland, the Bantu who settled in present Uganda include: the Baganda, the Banyoro, the Batoro, the Banyankole, the Bakiga, the Bafumbira, the Basoga, the Bagwere, the Banyole, the Bagisu, and the Basamia-Bagwe. Though there are striking similarities in language and customs among the different Bantu groups, each group has its own peculiarities in customs and other social arrangements.

## Effects of Bantu migrations

The coming of the Bantu to Uganda had many effects. The most obvious among such effects is that they led to the settlement and increased the population of eastern, central and southern Uganda. They are also credited with introducing ironworking in Uganda. Although it is not yet clear whether it was the Bantu or the legendary Bachwezi who introduced ironworking in Uganda, we still believe that the Bantu might have come with the idea because their movement coincided with the *Iron Age* (A.D 500–500 ).

It is also stated that the Bantu introduced centralised governments of the type that existed in the Bantu kingdoms of Buganda, Bunyoro-Kitara, Nkore and Toro, Igara and Buhweju. The assertion, however, has raised a number of theories. Some historians assert that the idea of centralised kingdoms was brought by the Luo. Other historians insist that the idea of centralised government could not have been an indigenous one. They attribute state formation to the Bachwezi whom they say were Hamites from Ethiopia who were of

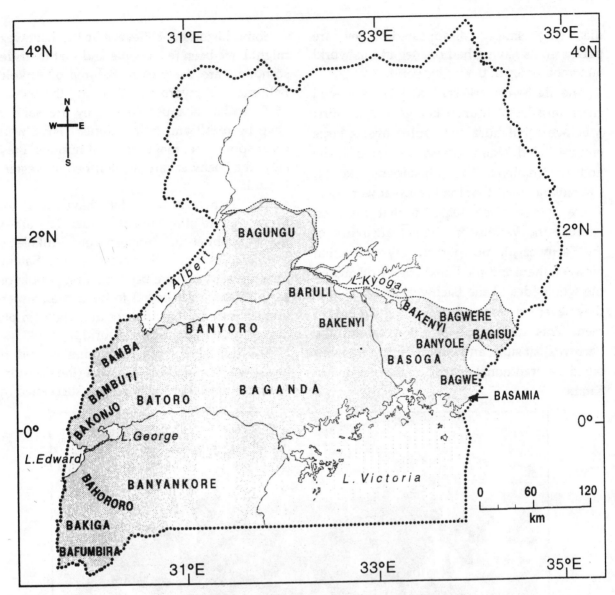

*Distribution of the Bantu Group*

either Portuguese or Greek origin. Such assertions are presently not taken very seriously because they contain a lot of bias against the idea of African initiative. It can therefore be tentatively stated that the Bantu brought the idea of centralised state formation while these assertions are subjected to further research.

The Bantu are also said to have introduced agriculture. This is true because their predecessors were essentially hunters and gatherers. In addition to agriculture, the Bantu also introduced crops such as millet and sorghum.

## The Bachwezi

The Bachwezi have been surrounded with obscurity. There is no agreement among historians about who they were, where they came from, what they brought, where they went, and where they are now.

Oral traditions from Bunyoro, Toro, Ankole, Rwanda and Karagwe where the Bachwezi are supposed to have settled, assert that they were demi-gods because even if they were born of men and women, they did not die. They simply disappeared. They are portrayed as having had one leg in this world and another leg in the underworld.

The Bachwezi are said to have assumed characteristics of human beings and the first Muchwezi, Ndahura, who ruled over a large empire called Kitara, is also venerated as the god of smallpox. Some historians like Fr. Crazzolara assert that the Bachwezi were Luo. There is not much sense in that assertion because the various traditional attributes of the Bachwezi do not portray any connection between them and the Luo. Wrigley dismissed the whole idea of the Bachwezi and says that they never existed at all except in the minds of men. This makes the traditions about the Bachwezi absurd and yet they are remembered as traditional rulers of the empire of Kitara.

Some historians believe that the Bachwezi might have been real people and that their descendants are the present Bahima of Ankole, Bahuma of Bunyoro and Toro and the Batutsi of Rwanda. In appearance, they are said to have been tall and light skinned. They were great sportsmen, magicians and hunters. Presently the Bachwezi are worshipped in western Uganda.

The Bachwezi are said to have ruled the Kitara empire after the Batembuzi. The era of the Batembuzi in Bunyoro and Ankole is conceived as a period of creation. The Batembuzi are said to have been the first people on earth. They are believed to have been superhuman because they did not die. They simply disappeared into the underworld.

The dynasty of the Batembuzi is said to have been founded by Ruhanga (the Creator). **Tradition says that Ruhanga was succeeded by**

*Ankole long-horned cattle: linked to Bacwezi*

his brother Nkya and Nkya was succeeded by his son Kakama. Bada succeeded his father Kakama and he is said to have been in turn succeeded by his son Ngonzaki. Ngonzaki was succeeded by his son Isaza, the last of the Batembuzi rulers. Before he disappeared in the underworld, Isaza is said to have impregnated Nyamate, the daughter of Nyamiyonga, king of the underworld. Nyamate gave birth to Isimbwa who in turn was the father of Ndahura, the first Muchwezi. This tradition presupposes that the Bachwezi were related to the Batembuzi.

The Bachwezi are said to have founded the ancient empire of Kitara. This empire is said to have covered the whole of central, western and southern Uganda; northern Tanzania; western Kenya and eastern Zaire. Their capital is said to have been on Mubende hill and then at Bigo Bya Mugyenyi in Masaka district. In all traditions, Bigo is linked with Mugyenyi who is said to have been a Muchwezi prince. Excavations at Bigo have revealed the existence of findings which are also associated with the ancient capital sites of Ankole and Buhaya such as Bwegorere and Bweranyangi respectively. These have also been excavated by archeologists. This proves at least, in part, that the Bachwezi were real people. However, the exact extent of the Kitara empire could not have stretched as far as is usually assumed. What can be said is that the Bachwezi had a loosely organised empire, not very small but at least not as big as is assumed; perhaps slightly bigger than the present central, western and southern Uganda, northwestern Tanzania, northern Rwanda and eastern Zaire. It was based in Bwera and along the middle banks of River Katonga.

When the Luo invaded Bunyoro at the beginning of the 16th century, the Bachwezi are said to have migrated southwards and left the Luo to establish their Babiito dynasty over the former Bachwezi empire of Kitara. According to traditions, the Bachwezi disappeared to an unknown destination. Some historians assert, however, that the Bachwezi might have been absorbed within the local populations and might in effect be the present Bahima and Batutsi of southern Uganda. The actual truth is yet to be established but the Bachwezi were pastoralists and are said to have had some physical features similar to those of the Bahima.

When the Bachwezi left, Bwera territory was left to a Mwiru smith called Kihesi. Kihesi is said to have made a drum called *Rushama* from waterbuck skin. Until recently, this drum was kept at Makore a few miles from Bigo. Kihesi is said to have acquired the name of *Bararemwa Kihasha Nantomu* and established the kingdom of Bwera.

## What the Bachwezi brought

As the exact origin, nature and presence of the Bachwezi is still open to question, their introductions and other attributes are also still questionable. It is said that they introduced the long-horned Ankole cattle, the cultivation of coffee, the skills of iron smelting, games like wrestling and *mweso* and more importantly, the idea of kingdoms or centralised states in Uganda.

They are supposed to have brought with them the idea of kingship and kingly regalia and introduced the building of palaces and the employment of women at the kings' courts. A lot has been said for and against such assumptions but the Bachwezi are said to have inherited the Batembuzi dynasty. Wamala is said to have been the last Muchwezi king. Tradition says that Wamala and the remaining Bachwezi disappeared into a lake in Singo named after his name. Other historians simply state that the Bachwezi moved south and founded the kingdoms of Nkore, Rwanda and the Bahinda states of Karagwe.

*Two generations of traditional rulers of Uganda's four kingdoms: (Above left to right): Andereya Duhaga of Bunyoro; Daudi Chwa of Buganda; Sulmani Kahaya of Ankole; and Daudi Kyabambe of Toro. (Below, left to right): Sir Edward Mutesa of Buganda; Sir Charles Gasyonga of Ankole;  Sir Tito Winyi of Bunyoro, and Sir Rukidi George Agutamba of Toro.*

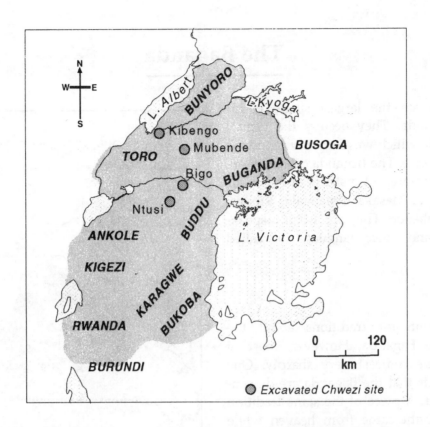

*The possible extent of the Chwezi Empire of Bunyoro-Kitara*

*A Ugandan family playing Mweso*

# The Baganda

The Baganda are the largest single ethnic group in Uganda. They occupy the central part of Uganda which was formerly called the Buganda province. The Baganda can therefore be found in the present districts of Kampala, Mpigi, Mukono, Masaka, Kalangala, Kiboga, Rakai and Mubende. They are a Bantu-speaking people and their language is. called Luganda.

## Origins

There are abundant traditions about the origins of the Baganda. However, most of these traditions contrast very sharply. One tradition asserts that the Baganda are descendants of Kintu. A piece of the same tradition claims that Kintu came from heaven while another piece asserts that he came from the east, from the direction of Mt. Elgon and passed through Busoga on his way to Buganda. Another tradition asserts that the Baganda are the descendants of a people who came from the east or the northeast round about A.D.1300. These people were either Hamites from Ethiopia or Luo from the Sudan. Sir Apollo Kaggwa's version says that the first Muganda was Kintu and that Kintu came from heaven and landed at Podi harbour in Bunyoro. From Podi, Kintu is said to have moved on to Kibiro and with his companions finally reached Kyadondo and founded the kingdom of Buganda. One could possibly gather that the Baganda came to occupy Buganda from two main directions: one from the east by way of Busoga and another from the west by way of Bunyoro. The best that can be said is that being Bantu speaking, the Baganda originated from central Africa where all the Bantu are said to have originated.

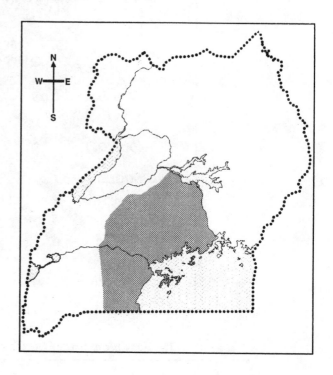

## Religion

The Baganda believed in superhuman spirits in the form of *mizimu, misambwa* and *Balubaale*. The Balubaale were believed to have been men whose exceptional attributes in life were carried over into death. The mizimu were believed to be ghosts of dead people for it was believed that only the body would die and rot but the soul would still exist as *omuzimu* (singular of *mizimu*). Such ghosts were believed to operate at the family level to haunt whoever the dead person had a grudge with. If the mizimu entered natural objects, they were believed to become misambwa. At another level, the mizimu could become tribal figures and also be known as Balubaale.

The supreme being among the Baganda was the Creator, *Katonda*. Katonda was, believed to have had neither children nor

*Wanema's temple (one of Buganda's gods) in Sese Islands*

parents. He was said to have created the heavens and the earth with all that they contain. Katonda was however, not believed to be very different from the other Balubaale. In fact he was believed to be one of the seventy-three Balubaale in Buganda. There were three temples for Katonda in Buganda and all of them were situated in Kyaggwe under the care of priests from the *Njovu* clan.

The other Balubaale had specific functions. The most important among them were: Katonda, Ggulu, god of the sky and the father of Kiwanuka, god of lightning. Then there was Kawumpuli, god of plague, Ndaula, god of smallpox, Musisi; god of earthquakes, Wamala, god of Lake Wamala; and Mukasa, god of Lake Victoria. Musoke was the god of the rainbow and Kitaka was the god of the earth.

There were temples dedicated to the different Balubaale throughout Buganda. Each

temple was served by a medium and a priest who had powers over the temple and acted as a liaison between the Balubaale and the people. In particular clans, priesthood was hereditary, but a priest of the same god could be found in different clans. The priests occupied a place of religious importance within society and they usually availed themselves for consultation.

The kings had special shrines of worship. The royal sister known as *Nnaalinya* took charge of the king's temple. There is a tradition among the Baganda that the Balubaale cult was introduced by Kabaka Nakibinge to strengthen his authority and that he combined both political and religious functions for that matter.

## Marriage

The Baganda regarded marriage as a very important aspect of life. A woman would

*Traditional bridal attire made from barkcloth*

normally not be respected unless she was married. Nor would a man be regarded as being complete until he was married. And the more women a man had the more of a man he would be regarded. This presupposes indeed that the Baganda were polygamous. A man could marry five wives or more provided he could manage to look after them. It was easier to become polygamous in Buganda than in other parts of Uganda because the bride-wealth obligations were not prohibitive. However, unlike in other societies of Uganda, divorce was very common in Buganda.

Formerly parents would initiate and conduct the marriage arrangements for their children. A father could, for instance, choose a husband for his daughter and the daughter would not question whether the husband chosen was too old, too young or unappealing. It was common for old men to marry young

girls to rejuvenate themselves. However, as time passed, boys could make their choices and, with the help of their families, proceed to make formal arrangements for marriage. The girl would contribute nothing more than her consent. After the due introductions and the payment of the appropriate bridewealth a formal ceremony would be arranged and the girl would be officially handed over for marriage. Such ceremonies were great occasions of eating, drinking, dancing and social gathering. A man could not marry from his own clan except for the members of the *Mamba* and *Ngabi* clans. They gave the simple justification that they were very many. Even then marriages occurred between distant clan members.

The formal arrangements were such that the girl's aunt would dress her smartly and the boy would be invited to look at her. If the boy appreciated her, further arrangements would be made for introductions. Following the introductions, more arrangements were made for the payment of the bridewealth and then the handover ceremony. If the girl was a virgin, she would be escorted by her aunt. If she was not, the aunt as an escort would not go. The purpose of the aunt would be to take the bedding and a goat that had never had sexual relations with a he-goat. On her way out, she would pass by the rear door of the house. On reaching home, the goat was slaughtered and eaten without salt.

## Death

The Baganda feared death very much. They did not believe in such paradigms as life after death. Whenever someone died, they would weep and wail round the corpse. Weeping was important because one who did not weep and wail could easily be suspected of causing the deceased's death. The Baganda did not believe that death was a natural consequence. All deaths were attributed to wizards, sorcerers and supernatural spirits. Therefore, after almost every death, a witch doctor would be consulted.

Burial was usually after five days. The body had to wait for that long in the belief that it might still contain the element of life and might perhaps come back to life. Some people, especially the women would even go as far as pinching the corpse to ascertain if it could feel the pain. Women were believed to rot faster than men and they were thus normally buried earlier than men. After burial, there would follow a month of mourning; ten days after mourning would be funeral rites known as *okwabya olumbe*.

Okwabya olumbe was a great ceremonial feast whereby all the clan elders would be invited and many people would attend. It involved a lot of eating, drinking, dancing and unrestrained sexual intercourse among the members present. On that same occasion, an heir would be installed if the deceased was the head of the family. The heir apparent would stand near the door dressed in ceremonial barkcloth and armed with a spear and a stick.

*Baganda mourners at the burial of Kabaka Mutesa II in 1971*

The elders would then instruct him as appropriate and require him, among other things, to assist the beneficiaries. The children of the deceased would be covered with barkcloth and told to go crying to the plantation in order that the ghost of the deceased should come out of the home. They were also required to shave off their hair.

## Birth

Whenever a woman was pregnant, she would use a herb called *nalongo* in order that her pubic regions should widen. If a woman had ever given birth, she would begin to use the herb at the seventh month of pregnancy. If she was conceiving for the first time, she would begin using it during the sixth month of pregnancy.

After giving birth, the *kigoma* (afterbirth) was buried near the doorway. The essence of burying it was to remove it from the reach of those who might employ it for evil purposes such as killing the child or rendering the mother barren. The mother would spend three days in confinement after birth but the period tended to depend on when the umbilical cord got dry. After about two weeks, the husband would play sex with the wife for the first time after she had given birth. This was a ritual function connected with the health of the child, and on that day, the child would be named. Thereafter the woman would stay celibate for some time before resuming sexual intercourse with the husband.

## Social stratification

Unlike the neighbouring societies of Ankole, Bunyoro and Toro, the Baganda seem to have been a coherent group. The society provides a striking example of being one with no fixed social divisions. The society was so fluid that any person of talent and ability could rise to a position of social importance. But this did not mean that the Baganda society had no classes as such because at any one time, the distinction between one class and another could be made.

At the bottom of the social stratum, there was a class of people known as the *Bakopi* (serfs). Fallers described *mukopi* as "simply a person who did not matter". The Bakopi obtained their livelihood from the goodwill of the *Baami* (chiefs) and the *Balangira* (princes), the other two social groups in Buganda. They depended on land but they had no rights to it. Therefore, a mukopi was almost a serf to the *mwami* or the *Kabaka*.

In ascending order, the next class in the Baganda society were the chiefs or the Baami as they were called. The Baami were not born Baami as a class but they could become such through distinguished services and ability or just by royal appointment. The Baami were a middle class in Buganda society. In fact the fluidity of the Kiganda system is evidenced by the class of the Baami. Initially, the status of the Baami was enjoyed by the *Bataka* (clan

heads). However, after 1750, the men of the Bakopi class began to be promoted to become Baami. The Baami could be distinguished into three patterns namely the *Bakungu*, the *Bataka*, and the *Batongole*.

The highest class in Buganda society was the *Balangira*. This was the aristocracy who based their right to rule on royal blood. At any one time, society would recognise: the Kabaka; the queen mother variously referred to as *Namasole*, *Nabijano*, or *Kanyabibambwa*; then *Nalinya* popularly known as *Lubuga* (royal sister); then the *Katikiro* and the *Kimbugwe*. The group formed a class of its own in Buganda.

## Social characteristics

The original Baganda are said to have been short and stocky with a distinct big and flat nose. These characteristics can still be traced among the Baganda today, but generally, they have lost their original structure. This is mainly because of their ability to assimilate

*A Muganda elder prostrating before Prince Ronald Mutebi in 1992*

(Above): *An old Muganda man playing a lyre* (entongoli). (Below): *Young Baganda girls dancing to a traditional tune*

other peoples. Many people from Rwanda, Burundi, Ankole, Toro, and Busoga have been assimilated over time to become Baganda and they are proud of it.

The Baganda are generally proud of their society and they are always ready to welcome those that are interested in joining them. They tend to believe that their culture is superior to those of the other peoples of Uganda and they often look down upon their neighbours. Their sense of superiority was whetted by colonialism when the British made them their allies in subjugating other people and thereafter gave them a special status within the Protectorate of Uganda.

They tend to be polite but particular in their behaviour and actions. In greeting, their women kneel down as a sign of respect. Rarely could a Muganda pass another by without greeting him or her and they tended to be particular in their dress and walking. The Baganda were generally particular in their homes and in cooking. Strict rules would surround eating and they would all sit down on a mat, male and female alike. The male sat on one side while the female sat with legs bent backwards. None, it is said, could leave the dining ground before all had finished and without saying "Ofumbye nnyo" to the person who prepared the meal and "Ogabude" to the head of the family.

## Economy

The Baganda were essentially agriculturalists. The main crops grown included bananas, sweet potatoes, cassava, yams, beans, cowpeas and a wide assortment of green vegetables. They also kept chickens, goats, sheep and cattle.

Land was an asset of economic importance and all land was supposed to belong to the *Kabaka* (king). The Kabaka could grant and remove land to and from anyone and at any time without notice. The grant of land went hand in hand with the grant of a political

*Traditional attire of the Baganda*

*Modern attire of the Baganda*

office such as a Saza chief, Gombolola chief or Muluka chief. The chief would then grant the land to the people under his jurisdiction for cultivation. But the land in effect, still belonged to the Kabaka. If any chief lost political power, he would also lose the control of the land.

This presupposes that land was not only an asset of economic importance but also of political importance. The Kabaka used land as an instrument for winning the loyalty of his chiefs. The chiefs tended to remain loyal to the Kabaka for fear that the loss of chieftainship would also mean the loss of land and the loss of the rent extracted from the Bakopi (peasants).

Each clan was allocated some land known as *obutaka* on which to bury their dead. Such land was vested in the *Bataka* (clan heads). The general system of land tenure was feudal and very exploitative to the Bakopi. As a price for cultivating the land, they had to give part of the produce to the chiefs as *obusuulu* and *envujjo*.

*A Muganda woman in traditional barkcloth attire*

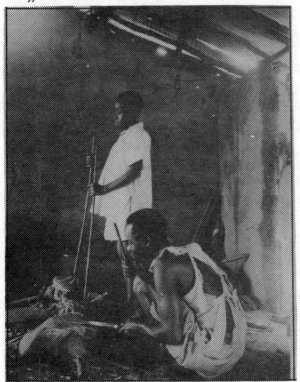

*Baganda blacksmiths making spears*

In 1900, this system of land tenure was slightly altered by the colonial government. All land in Buganda was divided into crown land and *mailo* land. Crown land was said to be the property of Her Majesty, the Queen of England and Ireland while mailo land was granted freehold to the chiefs and members of the Kabaka's family. This time the Bataka (clan heads) were not considered. The Bakopi retained their former position but exploitation intensified until 1927 when the *Busuulu* and *Nvujjo* were outlawed.

The Baganda were also skilled in creating works of art. Among them were excellent craftsmen, barkcloth makers, weavers and potters. They made excellent mats and a variety of baskets, pots and chairs. The best barkcloth makers in present Uganda could be found in Buganda. They also made spears, shields, bows and arrows. Among other

*A Muganda woman weaving a mat*

things, they also make drums of various shapes and sizes are made as well as many other musical instruments such as *endingidi*. The Baganda were also good at fishing and hunting. Most of the household work and cultivation was left to women while men concentrated on fighting, hunting and fishing. All these activities have nevertheless come under severe competition with modern industrial production processes. Industrial products have seriously undermined the skills and markets for crafts although some are still visible in many areas of the country.

In the later times, towards the middle of the 18th century, Buganda usurped the position of Bunyoro as the centre of the interlacustrine trade. They would trade in ivory, dried bananas, white ants, pottery and other crafts with the people of the interlacustrine region and with the coastal Arabs from the mid-19th century. When the colonialists arrived in the 1890's the Baganda readily supported them and adopted a new mode of economy based on trade and cash crop production. Presently,

the Baganda are among the richest people of Uganda.

## Political set-up

The Baganda had a centralised system of government which by 1750 was the most well organised in the interlacustrine region. The head of the state was the king known as *Kabaka*. Previously the Bataka had a lot of political influence. They enjoyed a position almost similar to that of Kabaka although they were subject to him in his capacity as *Ssabataka*. However after 1750, the Kabaka assumed a position of political importance far superior to the ranks of the Bataka. The Kabaka's position was hereditary but it was not confined to any one clan because the king would take the clan of his mother. The Kabaka used to marry from as many clans as possible and this encouraged loyalty to the throne in the sense that each of the fifty-two clans hoped that it would one day produce the king.

The other persons who occupied positions of political and social importance were: the Prime Minister known as the *Katikiro*, the *Mugema*, the royal sister known as *Nalinya*, the Queen mother  known as *Namasole* and the Naval and Army commanders referred to as *Gabunga* and *Mujasi* respectively.

The kingdom was divided into administrative units known as *Amasaza* (counties) which were further sub-divided into *Amagombolola* (sub-counties), and these were sub-divided into parishes called *Emiluka* which were sub-divided into sub-parishes. The smallest unit was known as *Bukungu* which was more or less a village unit. All the chiefs at all levels were appointed by the Kabaka and they were directly responsible to him. He could appoint or dismiss any chief at will. After 1750, chieftainship was no longer hereditary. Chieftainship was accorded on clan basis but only to men of merit and distinguished service.

*Ronald Muwenda Mutebi II being carried shoulder high after being crowned 36th king of Buganda on July  31, 1993.*

There was a system known as *okusenga* where children of the Bakopi were sent to grow up at the chiefs' and the Kabaka's courts as a means of apprenticeship. Those who demonstrated their ability were rewarded with political appointments. The system involved a lot of servitude and hard work coupled with harsh treatment by the chiefs. In this way a person could rise through the chiefly hierachy from a commoner to the appointed Katikiro if his services proved exemplary.

## Succession

Formerly, there would be succession disputes after the death of the Kabaka. With time, however, structural modifications were made to avoid such disputes. The most ancient of such modifications was for the king to kill all his sons and leave only one of them who would inherit the throne after his death. This system was too crude to last. As time went on, the reigning king would nominate the one who would succeed him before he died. It is said that such a nomination would be adhered to as far as it was humanly possible. But the final decision in such a case lay in the hands of the *Katikiro*, the *Kimbugwe* (traditional saza chief of Buruli) and *Kasujju-Lubinga* (a chief traditionally appointed from the Lugave clan to look after the *Balangira Bengoma* – the heirs apparent). The other princes who were not heirs to the throne were known as *Mituba* and they were under the direct control of an old prince known as *Sabalangira*. By the 1900 agreement, this procedure was severely altered. The Kabaka was to be elected by the Lukiiko and approved by Her Majesty the Queen of England and Ireland, Empress of India, etc. These conditions however remained on paper. The choice of the last two kings, Mutesa II and his son Mutebi II were through nomination by their own fathers.

## Death of the Kabaka

Whenever the Kabaka died, his drums known as *Majaguzo* were taken away to a place of safety until a new Kabaka was appointed. These drums were under the guardianship of members of the Lugave clan. The sacred fire referred to as *Gombolola* which had been kept incessantly burning at the entrance of the palace during the lifetime of the Kabaka

*Centuries-old root at Buddo where Buganda kings are crowned*

*Kasubi tombs where Buganda kings are buried*

would be extinguished. It would be re-lit on the installation of a new Kabaka. Indeed the customary phrase to announce the death of a Kabaka was: *"Omuliro gwe Buganda Guzi-kidde"* meaning that "Buganda's fire has been extinguished".

This tradition of equating the king's lifetime with the burning fire was believed to have started during the reign of Kintu and to have continued until the flight of Mutesa II from Lubiri palace in 1966. The traditional keepers of this fire were styled as *Senkole* and *Musolo-za*. It was also customary to announce the death of the Kabaka with the phrase *"Agye omukono mu ngabo"* meaning: "He has let loose the shield".

## Burial of the Kabaka

When the Kabaka died, his body would be carefully wrapped in appropriate attire and placed in a room called *Twekobe*, inside the Kabaka's house. The two chiefs *Kangawo* (title for the county chief of Bulemezi) and *Mugerere* (county chief of Bugerere) would be put in immediate charge of the body. Before burial, the body would be embalmed for almost six months. The Baganda believed that the spirit of a man would always remain where his jawbone was. For this reason, the jawbone of the Kabaka was removed from the body before burial and a special shrine was built to house it.

# The Banyoro

The Banyoro live in western Uganda to the east of Lake Albert. They inhabit the present districts of Hoima, Masindi, and Kibale. They speak a Bantu language and their origins, like other Bantu, can be traced to the Congo region. The Banyoro lived in scattered settlements in the populated parts of their country and their homesteads were rarely more than shouting distance from one another. Politically, they were organised under a king (*Omukama*).

## Naming

A few months after a child was born, three months for a boy and four months for a girl, a simple ceremony would be held at which the child was given a personal name along with one of the traditional *mpaako* names. The name could be given by a parent, a grand-parent or some other relative. But if the father of the child was known and present, he had the last word. The names given differed considerably. A few of them were family names handed down in particular clans to commemorate, for example, a relative or some feature on the child or some circumstances surrounding the child's birth.

There were special names for twins and those immediately following them. However the majority of other names portrayed the state of mind of the persons who gave them. Most names were real words which are used in everyday speech. The general theme of the names rotated around the constant imminence of sorrow or death, the experience or anticipation of poverty and misfortune and the spite or hatred of one's neighbours.

The names which relate to sorrow and death included Tubuhwaire, Buletwenda, Bulimarwaki, Kabwijamu, Alijunaki, Tibanagwa and several others. The names associated with poverty include: Bikanga, Baligenda, Babyenda, Bagamba, etc. The names intended

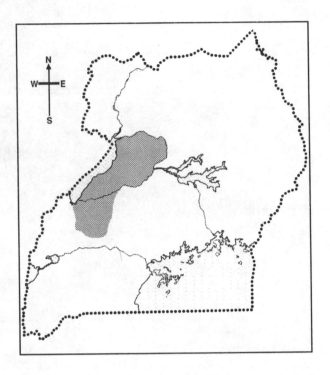

to portray the spite of neighbours included Itima, Tindyebwa, Nyendwoha, Nsekanabo, Ndyanabo, Tibaijuka and many others. Almost all the names portray that there were three things which the Banyoro feared very much, namely: death, sorrow and poverty.

## Greeting

The Banyoro used pet names *empaako* when greeting one another. These pet names are said to be of Luo origin and there are eleven in all. There are twelve if the word *Okali* is included but it is not empaako in the real sense. The real empaako are *Abwoli, Adyeri, Araali, Akiiki, Atwoki, Abooki, Apuuli, Bala, Acaali, Ateenyi* and *Amooti*.

When people who are related greet each other, the younger sits on the elder's lap. Among the Babiito, the young would also touch the elder's forehead and chin with their right-hand fingers. After the greeting, coffee berries specially kept for visitors would be brought and presented in a small basket for chewing. Thereafter, a tobacco pipe would be offered with tobacco for smoking.

## Greeting the Omukama (king)

The king was not greeted in the same way as ordinary people were greeted. Whenever he was in his residence, the king would sit in an advertised place for certain specified hours so that any of his subjects could go and see him. This practice of going to see the king was called *okukurata*. Whenever the people went to see the king they followed certain procedures and used a different language in addressing him.

There were more than twenty different ways of addressing the king at different times of the day. The king was not expected to reply to these greetings verbally, and he did not. Normally, in addressing the king, the third person singular was used. In fact nearly all verbs and nouns used to address the king were different from those that were used to address common men. However, women could kneel down and greet the king in the normal way and he would answer their greetings verbally.

## Marriage

The Banyoro were polygamous whenever they could afford it. Bridewealth was not so much of a prerequisite as it was in most societies of Uganda. In most instances, bridewealth could be paid later. Marriages were very unstable, divorce was frequent and there were many informal unions. In almost all cases, the survival of a marriage was not guaranteed. Payment of bridewealth was usually done after some level of stability in the marriage had been achieved. Often this would be after several years of marriage.

Traditionally, looking for a suitable partner was a matter involving the family of the boy and that of the prospective bride. The girl's contribution to the whole process amounted to nothing more than giving her consent. The first step was like it is today; a mutual attraction between the girl and the boy with a sexual relationship readily entered into. This was followed by the establishment of a domestic arrangement. Formalities of payment, if any, would normally follow but would not precede these arrangements. There was a tendency for boys to find girls from the same locality. In fact few would look for wives from beyond their villages.

## Death

The Banyoro feared death very much. Death was usually attributed to sorcerers, ghosts and other malevolent non-human agents. In some contexts, death was thought to be caused by the actions of bad neighbours. People were believed to be affected or harmed by gossip and slander. The Banyoro provided a vast range of magical and semi-magical means of injuring and even killing others. Indeed, many deaths were attributed to the act of sorcery by ill-wishers.

The Banyoro viewed death as a real being, like a person. Whenever a person died, old women of the household would close his eyes, shave his hair and beard, trim the finger nails and clean and wash the whole corpse. The body was left to remain in the house for a day or two with its face uncovered. The women and children were allowed to weep loudly but the men were not supposed to do so.

Whenever the head of a household died, some grains of millet mixed with simsim were placed in his right hand. This mixture was known as *ensigosigo*. Each of the dead man's children was required to take in his lips a small quantity of the mixture from the dead man's hand and eat it.

The body was wrapped in barkcloth, the number of the barkcloths depending on the wealth of the dead man. The following rites were performed by one of his nephews. The sister's son had to wrench out the central pole of the house and throw it into the middle of the compound. He would also take out the dead man's eating basket (*endiiro*) and his bow. The fire in the centre of the house was extinguished. There would be no fire for cooking in the house for the first three days of mourning.

A banana plant from the household's plantation with fruit on it was also brought and added to the heap of the dead man's utensils in the compound. Then the dead man's nephew or son would go to the well and bring some water in one of the household's water pots. On reaching the courtyard, he would break the water pot by throwing it down among the heap of the dead man's utensils. He had also to catch and kill the dead man's cock to prevent it from crowing. The chief bull's testicles were also ligatured at once to prevent it from engaging in any mating activity during the time of mourning. This bull would be slaughtered after four days and eaten. This act of killing male animals was known as *Mugabuzi*. The ceremony of killing and eating the main bull after four days concluded the period of mourning. The dead man's house would not be lived in again.

## Burial

In Bunyoro, burial would take place either in the morning or in the afternoon but not in the middle of the day. It was considered dangerous for the sun to shine directly into the grave. If the dead body was of a man, the last cloth on the corpse was wrapped around it in front of the house, in the doorway. If it was a woman, all this would be done inside the house.

When the body was being taken to the grave, women were required to moderate their weeping. At the grave, there would be no weeping. A pregnant woman was not supposed to attend a burial in the belief that she might miscarry. The body of a man was laid on its right side, that of a woman, on its left. These positions were correspondingly considered to be the appropriate ones to adopt when sleeping. In all cases, the head was placed towards the east and nobody was supposed to leave the graveyard before the burial was completed.

Before the burial took place, the grave was guarded otherwise it might demand another person. Should a grave be dug prematurely, and the supposedly dying person recovered, a banana plant was cut and buried in the grave.

After all burials, the hoe used to dig the grave was left by the grave-side with the basket used for removing the soil. People would wash themselves thoroughly and remove all the soil, for it was feared that if one walked in the garden with this soil on one's feet, the crops would wither and rot.

After the burial, people would cut hair from the back and front of their heads and throw it on the grave. The grave was marked with stones or iron rods because it was believed that if one built over a grave, all the members of his household might fall sick and die.

If a person died with grudges against anyone in the family, his mouth and anus would be stuffed with clay. This was supposed to prevent the ghost from coming out of the corpse to haunt those with whom the dead person had a grudge.

If a dead person was the head of the household, the grave digger would perform another ritual in which he would take a handful of a juicy plant and squeeze it with soot in his hands so that the juice ran down from his hands to the elbow. The children of the dead man were required to drink this juice from the elbow of the grave digger. On the day of the burial of the head of a household, a lot of firewood was placed in the middle of the compound. The children of the dead man would sit around it in turns. The grave digger would then tap each of the children on the side of the head with a large food basket. A small amount of hair from the part so tapped was cut off and thrown away.

## Political set-up

The Banyoro had a centralised system of government. At the top of the political leadership was the king (*Omukama*). His position was hereditary. He was the most important person in the kingdom. He was assisted in administrative matters by the provincial chiefs and a council of notables. The king was the commander-in-chief of the armed forces and each provincial chief was the commander of a military detachment stationed in his province. The king was assisted by a council of advisers known as the *Bajwara Nkondo* (wearers of crowns made from monkey skins).

There was a kind of political school in Mwenge; all the chiefs had to pass through it. Each chief had to send his favourite son to the king's court as a sign of allegiance. Leadership was not confined to men; the *Kogire* and *Nyakahuma* rulers of Busongora were women. Other persons of political importance in the kingdom were the *Bamuroga* (Prime Minister), the *Nyakoba* (a physician of the *Basuli* clan), *Kasoira Nyamumara* of the *Batwaire* clan and a leading *Mubiito*.

Bunyoro as a kingdom was initially bigger than the present districts of Hoima, Masindi and Kibale. The legendary kingdom of Bunyoro-Kitara from which the kingdom of Bunyoro emerged is said to have been a very big empire comprising the whole of present western Uganda, eastern Zaire, western Kenya and parts of northern Tanzania. This Bunyoro-Kitara empire was founded by the Bachwezi.

It is supposed to have collapsed at the advent of the Luo. The Biito Luo are said to have established the Babiito dynasty over some of the remains of the Bachwezi state.

The Babiito kingdom of Bunyoro-Kitara is said to have included present Hoima, Masindi, Mubende, Toro, Busigira, Bwera, Buddu, Buhweju, Kitagwenda and was sovereign over some parts of Busoga. However, over time the kingdom of Bunyoro-Kitara started to shrink. Due to frequent secession disputes, it became weak and fell prey to the expanding kingdoms of Buganda and Nkore. Bunyoro-Kitara was the biggest and strongest kingdom in the interlacustrine region by the beginning of the 18th century. However, by the end of the 18th century, Bunyoro-Kitara had become weak and started to lose some of her territory. The provinces of Butambala, Gomba, Buddu and Busoga were lost to Buganda. Some of her parts like Chope, Toro and Buhweju had earlier broken away and declared their own independence.

In 1869, Kabalega succeeded his father Kamurasi as the king of Bunyoro-Kitara and he tried to reorganise and reconquer the lost glory of Bunyoro-Kitara. He trained and equipped his new standing army (the *Abarusura*). He embarked on wars of recapture. He started with Toro, and then chope. As he was beginning to move against Buganda, the British colonialists arrived. They supported Toro and Buganda against Kabalega and defeated and exiled him to the Seychelles in 1899. Some of Bunyoro's provinces of Buyaga and Bugangaizi were given to Buganda. This left Bunyoro with only the present districts of Hoima and Masindi. The two counties were returned to Bunyoro after a referendum in 1964. The kingdom of Bunyoro was among the others abolished in 1967. With the restoration of traditional cultural institutions in 1993, Prince Solomon Iguru, a descendant of Kabarega , was installed as heir to the throne

*Sir Tito Winyi; King of Bunyoro*

*Bunyoro orunyegye dancers*

of Bunyoro. Unlike his ancestors, however, he is a cultural leader with no political and administrative power. Under his patronage, the Banyoro are striving to salvage and maintain what they can of their age-old culture.

### The new moon and *Empango* ceremonies

The Banyoro observed new moon ceremonies. During a new moon ceremony, people would assemble at the king's court to dance to the music which was provided by the royal bandsmen. This was to celebrate the Omukama's having lived to see the new moon.

The royal band which comprised about twenty men, performed at the ceremony. They participated in relays, playing drums, flutes and other wind instruments. The festivities of the new moon ceremony could go on for a few days at the king's palace.

There was also an annual celebration which used to go on for a period of nine days. This was arranged so that seven days would be celebrated at the king's mother's enclosure. This ceremony (*Empango*),was normally held in the dry season between December and January. During the colonial period this ceremony was modified and was celebrated once in three years for two or three days.

### Household and village set-up

The duties of political authority started from the household. In Bunyoro, the household was in effect a district. It was a kingdom ruled over by *Nyineka* (the family head). The status of Nyineka was ideally inherited by the eldest son in the event of death.

The village was politically organised so that the level of co-operation within it was much more pronounced than outside it. Each village had a specially recognised elder known as *Mukuru w'Omugongo*. He was selected from among the elders and he acted as an intermediary between them and the chiefs. Besides, he

*A Munyoro man transporting pots to the market*

had an informal court composed of himself and a few other elders. This court settled the village disputes.

## Economy

The Banyoro were a highly egalitarian society. Property was a criterion for distinguishing between superior and inferior persons. Land was an asset of economic importance and it was the basis of the Banyoro's economic activity. Their staple food included millet, potatoes, cassava, beans, meat and bananas. Certain foods were reserved for particular functions. For example, a guest's meal had to consist of millet and meat. Potatoes were never given to guests except in times of scarcity. A guest had to be given a meal at whatever time he

*Craftsman making a traditional mortar*

arrived, even if it was after midnight.

The society was stratified into the *Bairu*, *Bahuma* and the *Bakama*. The Bairu formed the majority of the population. They did different activities which were locally carried out. The year was divided into twelve months as follows:

During January (*Igesa*) they would be harvesting millet. In February (*Nyarakarwa*) they did not have much work. The month was referred to as the month of white ants. In March (*Ijubyamiyonga*), fields were prepared for planting simsim. In May (*Rwenseizere*) there was no much work. The month was also referred to as a month of white ants. During the month of July, (*Isanya Maro*) women would prepare fields for millet. August (*Ikokoba*) was a month of burning grass in the millet fields and September (*Isiga*) was for planting millet. November (*Rwensenene*) was named after grasshoppers but October (*Ijuba*) was a month for weeding. Lastly, December (*Nyamiganura* or *Katuruko*) was a month for rejoicing and festivities as there was little work to occupy the people.

During the pre-colonial days, Bunyoro was a centre of trade. There was salt trading from the salt deposits of Lakes Katwe, Kasenyi and Kibiro as well as iron-ore deposits near Masindi. The Banyoro were excellent iron-smiths and this attracted many societies to come to Bunyoro for trade. The Banyoro were also experts in making red-hoes, which were very much desired by the societies north of Lake Kioga, particularly the Langi and the Iteso.

# The Batooro

The Batooro inhabit the districts of Kabarole and Kasese. Their area has been infiltrated by many migrants from other parts of western Uganda, particularly the Bakiga. To their east live the Banyoro; to their north are the Bamba and the Bakonjo; to their southeast, and west live Banyankore and to their east live the Baganda. The Batooro are Bantu speaking. Their language is *Rutooro*.

## Origins

There exist conflicting legends about the origin of the Batooro. One legend asserts that the Batooro are indigenous to Toro and that they originated from the Batembuzi and the Bagabu who are said to have been the pioneer inhabitants and rulers of the earth. Some other traditions assert that the Batooro are related to the Bachwezi and the Babito line. What can best be said is that the Batooro, being Bantu, originated from the Congo region where the other Bantu groups are said to have originated.

## Social set-up

The Batooro society was stratified into the *Bahuma* and the *Bairu*. The relationship between the two was more of a caste rather than

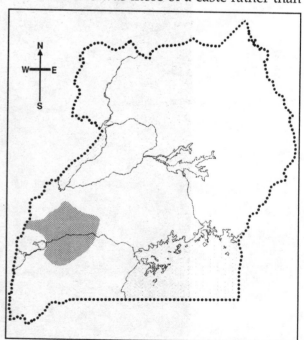

class differentiation. The Bahuma were pastoralists while the Bairu were agriculturalists. Socially and economically, there was a symbiotic relationship between the two people. The Bairu could get meat, milk, hides and other cattle products from the Bahuma and equally the Bahuma would get beer and some other agricultural products from the Bairu.

## Marriage

Marriage occupied an important position in the cultural life of the Batooro. A man would not be regarded as complete before he got married. Formerly, marriage could be arranged by the parents of both the boy and the girl with or without the knowledge and consent of either of them. During the preparations, however, the consent of the girl would have to be sought.

A middle-man was usually sought by the boy's side and his role was socially recognised and rewarded. He was known as *Kibonabuko*. He had the duty of making investigations about the character of the girl, her family background, and her ability to work. After such groundwork was completed, the Kibonabuko would proceed to secure the girl from her parents on behalf of the boy's family.

The Kibonabuko would wake up one morning and go to the girl's family to declare his intention to marry their daughter. He would make the following statement to the father of the girl:

Sir, I come to you to ask that you should build a house for me. I would like you to be part of my clan; I have come to ask for a wife, the builder of the house.

The normal response from the girl's father was: "I don't have any child". The Kibonabuko would insist that the child was there, and on being asked who exactly he wanted, he would name the girl. If the father consented, the Kibonabuko would thankfully kneel down, as

*A modernised traditional Toro costume*

a sign of appreciation. The next step would then be for the boy's family to take beer to the girl's parents to have the bridewealth fixed.

The bridewealth was normally in the form of cows. It varied between the Bahuma and Bairu. For the Bahuma, it ranged from six to twenty cows. For the Bairu, the ceiling was about eight cows. They could often make payments in goats and hoes. All or part of the bridewealth when due, would be received during a ceremony known as *okujuga*. It was a very important ceremony involving a lot of eating, drinking and merrymaking. Thereafter, the young man's family could send barkcloth and some skins for the bride's dress. Meanwhile other formalities would be finalised for the wedding.

On the wedding day, another big feast was organised. The bride would be collected around six or seven o'clock in the evening. Before leaving, she would first perform the ritual of siting on her parents' laps. This ritual was known as *okubukara*. She would then be lifted onto a litter and carried to the bridegroom's home. On arrival, she would perform the ritual of sitting on the laps of her parents-in-law. There she would be sprinkled with some herbal water (*endembezi*) to welcome and bless her. Before the feasting started, the bridegroom would go to bed with the bride, to perform another ritual, *okucwa amagita*. Thereafter, the guests were given coffee berries, smoking pipes, beer and, later, food. If the girl was found to be a virgin in the process of okucwa amagita, a gift of a cow or a goat would be sent to her mother to congratulate her on raising her daughter well. On the fourth day the bride's friends and relatives would bring her gifts from home. They would come to see where she had been taken. The bride would spend some days in confinement and, at the end of it all, an elaborate ceremony would be held to bring the girl out and to initiate her into the art of cooking and housekeeping.

In the event of a divorce bridewealth would be refunded. However, part of the bridewealth would be retained if the woman had already had some children with her husband.

## Religion

The Batooro had a concept of a supreme being called Ruhanga. Ruhanga was believed to have created all things. He was believed to be a good and benevolent being who, unless wronged, could not do harm to the people. However, it was believed that the world was full of evildoers, evil spirits and sorcerers who could employ their magic to undermine Ruhanga and cause disease, misfortune, barrenness, death and droughts or even bad weather.

The Batooro believed that there existed mediums some of whom were agents of the devil while the good ones were the agents of Ruhanga. The Batooro also believed in the *mandwa* cult. Shrines were constructed for the worship of *emandwa* in every home. The mandwa were usually worshipped and praised by playing *entimbo* (drums and trumpets). In the actual process of worship people would wear skins (*emikako*) knitted with beads and cowrie shells. An important medium of the mandwa would wear a six centimetre bark-cloth material with horns on the head (*ekisingo*). The whole process of worshipping involved a lot of eating and drinking.

In the event of disease, death or misfortune, a *mufumu* (diviner) would be consulted to interpret the demands of emandwa. Thereafter, appropriate measures would be taken to appease the mandwa. Supplications to the mandwa were normally effected at night. A man would put fire in front of the house and pronounce his problems to the mandwa. The language used in addressing emandwa was slightly different from the common one used in ordinary parlance. The pronunciation of certain words was slightly altered. Surprisingly, in talking to emandwa the Batooro would use Runyankole terminologies. For instance *omukama* was pronounced as *omugabe*, *okurora*, as *okureeba*, *omwaana omwerere*, and several others.

## Greeting

Besides their family names, the Batooro, like the Banyoro have pet names called *empaako*. These pet names are said to be of Luo origin although the Luo themselves do not use them. Empaako was a sign of social identity. When greeting each other, the Batooro use the empaako. When people who were related greeted each other, the younger would sit on the lap of the elder. Among the Babiito, the younger would touch the forehead and chin of the elder before announcing the empaako.

## Blood brotherhood

The Batooro, like their Banyankore neighbours, practised blood brotherhood, but a man could also make blood brotherhood with a woman. The main ingredients of the ceremony included coffee berries, a new barkcloth, a knife, two branches of a fig tree and sprouts of a grass called *ejubwe*. The climax of the ceremony was the taking, with coffee berries of one's blood from a cut made just below the navel. Then the two blood brothers would take an oath to behave as real brothers in all respects. Two men and one old woman would usually act as witnesses to the occasion.

The two celebrants would pronounce the following words to each other during the ceremony:

Brothers fight and shave each other; they cut each other's nails; they beat each other and help each other.

If you become dishonest to me, your stomach will swell. When I come to you with a horrible disease, you will not send me away. When I come naked, you will not send me away. When I come to your home, I will not go away hungry. We shall not do evil to each other, nor shall our children and clans.

*A milking ritual in Toro palace*

## Economy

The economy of Batooro was partly agricultural and partly pastoral. The Bahuma were pastoralists while the Bairu were agriculturalists. Cows were much valued by both groups and, besides providing milk and beef, cattle were a symbol of wealth.

The Batooro cultivated millet, sorghum, bananas, peas, and a variety of green vegetables. They also had local industries to produce iron implements such as spears, hoes, knives, and arrowheads, bark-cloth and salt. Besides, they also had a number of potters who produced a variety of household utensils such as water pots, beer pots and sauce pots.

The women were good at basket weaving and they produced a wide assortment of basketry such as winnowing trays, plate baskets, bags, harvesting baskets and several baskets for routine household work. The men constructed houses, cleared bushes and hunted wild animals. Certain activities like hunting and house construction were done on a communal basis. House construction involved eating, drinking and dancing. Batooro built circular huts with grass-thatched roofs.

## Political set-up

The Batooro had a centralised system of government. Toro had until 1830 been a part of Bunyoro. In 1830, Prince Kaboyo declared Toro independent of Bunyoro and reorganised it into another kingdom.

At the head of the kingdom was a king known as *Omukama*, the first being Kaboyo Kasusunkwanzi, the actual founder of the

*Omukama Patrick Olimi-Kaboyo at a ritual function during the restoration of the kingdom of Toro, 1993*

(Above): *Omukama Rukidi, after a church service to mark his coronation anniversary.*
(Below): *Omukama Rukidi of Toro at a spear ceremony.*

*Toro royal throne*

kingdom. He was succeeded by his son, Nyaika who was in turn succeeded by Kasagama. Kasagama ruled until he was dethroned by Kabalega of Bunyoro but was later reinstated in 1891 by Captain Lugard, an agent of Imperial British East African Company (IBEA Co.) which was trying to extend British imperialism to Uganda.

The king was hereditary and he had to be from the Babiito dynasty which was ruling Bunyoro. He was assisted by a hierarchy of chiefs and a standing army. But in times of war all able-bodied men would be called upon to serve in the defence of the kingdom. The chiefly regalia included drums, spears, iron-forks, wooden spoons and chairs, crowns, skins, mats, beads, axes and knives.

The county of Mwenge was of particular importance in the kingdom. It contained a school of political education when Toro was still part of Bunyoro. When Toro broke away from Bunyoro, Mwenge retained this function. The sons of the kings were sent to Mwenge to learn the art and the language of government. It is said that there were also special tutors for the king's daughters. When the king's wives were about to give birth they would be sent to

*A Mutooro royal drummer*

Mwenge. Rebellious princes were also sent to a political school in Mwenge and it is perhaps because of the political and social importance of Mwenge that no war was fought in Mwenge.

The Toro kingdom suffered the same fate as those of Bunyoro, Buganda and Ankole with the advent of republicanism in 1967. However, the institution of Omukama was reinstated in 1993 albeit without its former political and administrative powers. Omukama Olimi Kaboyo was installed as the fifth Omukama of Toro. He reigns as the cultural head of the Batooro.

# The Bakonjo and Bamba

## Origins

The Bakonjo and Bamba are Bantu and they are said to have a common origin with the other Bantu groups. The Bakonjo are found in the district of Kasese. They are the most numerous of the Rwenzori peoples, being more than either the Bamba or the Bambuti. Physically they are generally short and stout. Legend has it that the Bakonjo once lived on Mt. Elgon in eastern Uganda and that during the Kintu migrations, the Bakonjo came with Kintu and the other peoples to Buganda. However, rather than settle in Buganda, the Bakonjo are said to have decided to continue until they finally settled on the western highlands of Mt. Rwenzori which had a climate similar to that of Mt. Elgon where they had originally lived. This is said to have been around A.D.1300. Another tradition asserts that the Bakonjo have lived on Mt. Rwenzori from time immemorial and that they have no foreign place of origin. This tradition asserts that the ancestor of the Bakonjo emerged from one of the caves of Mt. Rwenzori and produced the rest of the Bakonjo. This tradition, however, is too simplistic to be generally accepted. What could best be said is that since the Bakonjo are Bantu speaking, they could trace their origin to the Congo region where the other Bantu groups originated.

## Marriage

Marriage among the Bakonjo and Bamba was a matter of great social concern. It was usual

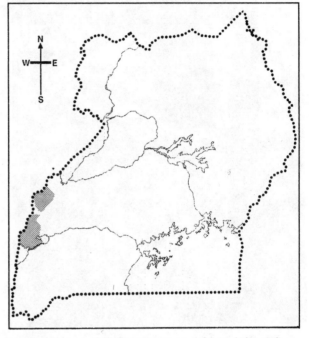

for families to book spouses early in life. Often the booking would be done on the day the boy was initiated. No marriage could be socially recognised unless bridewealth obligations had been settled. The bridewealth was normally paid in the form of goats. The number of goats was determined by the economic status of the families concerned. In addition to the number of goats, a digging stick and an animal skin had to be included. The digging stick would replace the girl's lost labour and the skin would replace one used by the girl when young. In modern times, a hoe and a blanket have replaced the digging stick and the skin. Divorce was rare but in the event of it, all the goats given as bridewealth would be paid back. All unmarried girls were supposed to be virgins. If a girl conceived before marriage she would be executed.

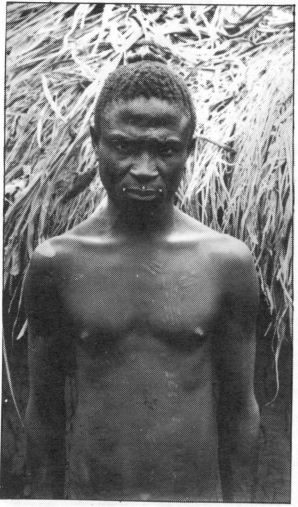

*Bamba: body marks*

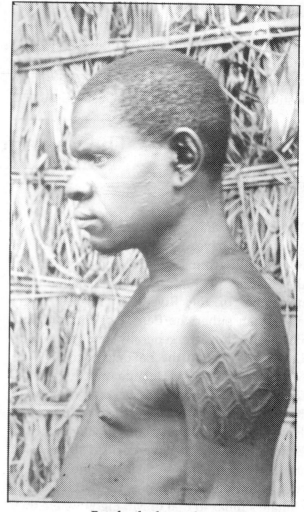

*Bamba: body marks*

## Initiation

The Bakonjo share some elements of culture with the Bamba. One such element was initiation. The purpose of initiation was to transform the initiates from childhood to adulthood. Therefore all the male children, before or after reaching puberty, had to undergo circumcision. This was conducted jointly by the Bakonjo and the Bamba. The ceremony would normally begin in Bwamba and then end in Bukonjo. The initiation ceremony was conducted after long intervals, often fifteen to seventeen years. It involved all male children from the age of three years.

## Religion

The Bakonjo believed in two supreme beings: *Kalisa* and *Nyabarika*. Kalisa was viewed as a monster with one arm, one eye, one leg, one ear, half a nose and half the rest of the body. Kalisa was a half man. The exact structure of *Nyabarika* is not known. He is believed to be the most powerful spiritual being. He had the power to heal, kill, haunt, provide fertility or cause barrenness and, indeed, make hunting expeditions successful or otherwise. Therefore, Nyabarika had to be pleased. Kalisa was regarded as being very important mainly with respect to hunting. Since hunting was a cherished occupation among the Bakonjo, one can tell the power and importance of Kalisa too.

On the southern and eastern slopes of the Rwenzori mountains, the Bakonjo used to construct shrines dedicated to Kalisa and Nyabarika. Such shrines would be made of bamboo sheaths. They were too small for a man to enter. They are said to have been numerous in the bamboo zones of the Nyamagasani and Nyamwamba rivers. They were rare in Mubuku and Bujuku valleys. The shrines were huts built in pairs. The larger huts were slightly over one metre high. A food offering of *matooke* or chicken, was placed on the stakes between the two huts.

## Hunting

Hunting was a very important activity among the Bakonjo. Although it was enjoyed as sport, more importantly, it was a source of food. Skilled hunters occupied a place of importance in the society. The main instruments of hunting included spears, hunting nets, bows and arrows and ropes. The Bakonjo also kept dogs.

Hunting was done on a small as well as large scale. Hunters included trappers who operated as individuals; occasional hunters in groups of two or as individuals; but the most interesting and well-organised hunters formed hunting troops. The troops could consist of as many as thirty to sixty people. There were rules and regulations concerning the conduct of the hunting expeditions and the sharing of the meat.

Before setting off on a hunting trip, supplications and sacrifices were offered to Kalisa and Nyabalika for the success of the hunting expedition. If the expedition was successful, some pieces of the meat were left at the slaughtering place. A small fence of bamboo stakes was constructed across the hunting path to bar any angry spirits from following the hunting party. Should a person use the path, he would cast a handful of green leaves over the bamboo stakes so that the said spirits would not follow him.

*Rwenzori mountains: home of the Bakonjo and Bamba*

## Secret communications

The Bakonjo had a system of secret communication used within families. This art was
strictly a father to son affair. The conversation
was done through whistling. The whistling
was of a peculiar quality, not loud but deeply
penetrating. This method of communication
was used during hunting to convey messages
like: "The animals are trying to turn back";
"The dogs have been sent for";  "The monkeys
have come to the ground on the other side of
the river". Messages could go as far as one
kilometre away. This type of communication
is said to have been so peculiar to the Bakonjo
that their immediate neighbours, the Bamba
and the Batooro, could not understand it.

## Economy

The Bakonjo are agriculturalists. They grow
mainly *matooke*, yams, potatoes, cassava and

*Bakonjo boys playing a flute*

*A Mukonjo stool maker*

beans. At a later time they took up coffee and cotton growing. In addition, they rear goats, sheep and fowls. Production was initially for subsistence and they supplemented their produce by hunting and fishing on Lakes Edward and George.

# The Banyankore

The Banyankore are a Bantu group. They inhabit the present districts of Mbarara, Bushenyi and Ntungamo in western Uganda. People from the present counties of Rujumbura and Rubabo in Rukungiri District share the same culture. Originally, Ankole was known as *Kaaro-Karungi* and the word *Nkore* is said to have been adopted during the 17th century following the devastating invasion of *Kaaro-Karungi* by Chwamali, the then Omukama of Bunyoro-Kitara. The word *Ankole* was introduced by the British colonial administrators to describe the bigger kingdom which was formed by adding to the original Nkore, the former independent kingdoms of Igara, Sheema, Buhweju and parts of Mpororo.

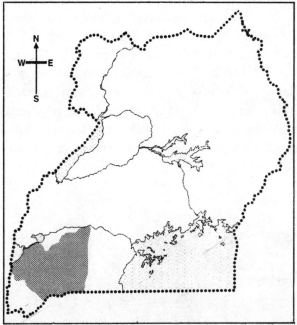

## Origins

Like other Bantu groups, the origins of the Banyankore could be traced to the Congo region. Legends hold that the first occupant of Ankole was *Ruhanga* (the Creator), who is said to have come from heaven to rule the earth. Ruhanga is said to have come with his three sons Kairu, Kakama and Kahima. There is a story about how Ruhanga gave a test to determine which of his three sons would become the heir. The test is said to have been that of keeping milk-filled pots on their laps throughout the night. At the end of it all, the youngest son, Kakama, is said to have passed the test followed by Kahima and last came the eldest son, Kairu. Judging from the performance in the test, Ruhanga is said to have decreed that Kairu and Kahima would serve their brother Kakama. Thereafter he went back to heaven, leaving Kakama or Rugaba, as he was also called, to rule the land. This legend portrays social stratification in Ankole society. It was concocted so as to make the Bairu accept their subservient position to the Bahima as being supernatural.

## Social stratification

The Banyankole society was stratified into the *Bahima* (pastoralists) and the *Bairu* (agriculturalists). A caste-like system of the Bahima over the Bairu existed. The society was a dual pyramid with pastoral and agricultural legs. Within the two groups or castes (I call them castes not classes because within the Bahima and the Bairu, there were those who had much in common), the clans cut across both the Bairu and the Bahima. The two groups recognised a common ancestry. There was a general belief that what made a *Mwiru* (singular of Bairu) what he is was a hoe and what made a *Muhima* (singular of Bahima) what he is was cattle. This kind of belief was not very accurate because merely acquiring cows would not immediately transform one from a Mwiru into a Muhima nor would the loss of cows transform a Muhima into a Mwiru. A Muhima who owned few cattle would be called a *Murasi*. A mwiru who owned cattle was called a *Mwambari*.

The two groups lived together and they depended on each other. The Bairu exchanged cattle products with Bahima and the Bahima equally received agricultural goods from the Bairu. This was because the Bairu needed milk, meat, hides and other cattle products from the Bahima while the Bahima would also need agricultural products from the Bairu, especially local beer.

## Marriage

Traditionally, the normal pattern was for the parents of both the boy and girl to arrange the marriage, sometimes without the knowledge of the girl concerned. The initiative was normally taken by the boy's parents and upon the payment of an appropriate bridewealth, arrangements would be made to fetch the bride. Customarily, a girl could not be offered for marriage when her elder sister, or sisters were still unmarried. If a marriage offer was made for a young sister, it is said that the girl's parents would manipulate issues in such a way that at the giving–away ceremony, they would conceal and send the elder sister. When

*A Muhima girl: hair decorations*

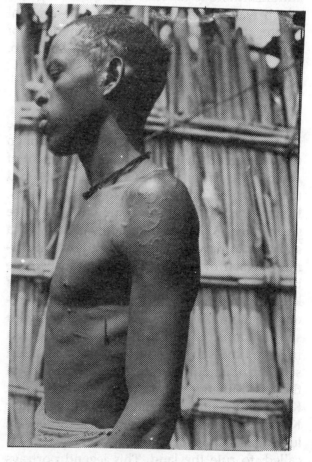

*A Muhima boy: body marks*

the bridegroom would come to know it he was not supposed to raise questions. He could go ahead to pay more bridewealth and then marry the younger sister if he could afford it. It was the responsibility of the father to pay in full the bridewealth and meet all the other costs of arranging his son's marriage.

During the wedding ceremony, the girl would be accompanied by among others, her aunt. Some traditions assert that the husband would first have sex with the aunt before proceeding to have it with the bride. Another piece of tradition says that the duty of the aunt was to prove the potency of the bridegroom by just watching or listening to the sexual intercourse between the bridegroom and her niece. It is also said that her duty was to advise the girl on how to begin a home more so, since, in Ankole, girls were supposed to be virgins until marriage. The first tradition is false because in most cases the aunt would be an elderly lady almost the same age as the

*A decorated hut, usually for receiving a bride*

*A pastoral Hima homestead*

mother of the bridegroom but the other two traditions are true. If the parents of the girl were aware that their daughter was not a virgin, this information was formally communicated to the husband by giving the girl, among other gifts, a perforated coin or another hollow object.

## Oruhoko

*Okuteera oruhoko* was a phrase used to describe the practice whereby a boy whom the girls had deliberately refused to love or whom a particular girl had rejected could force the girl to marry him abruptly without her consent and much preparation.

The practice of okuteera oruhoko was characteristic of the traditional Ankole society but vestiges of it still appear. Society decried this practice but it was common and helpful, nonetheless. However, the offender had to be fined by paying a big bridewealth. There were various ways in which this practice was carried out.

One such ways was by using a cock. A boy who had desired and wished to marry a girl who had rejected him, would get hold of a cock, go to the girl's homestead, throw the cock in the compound and then run away. The girl had to be whisked to the boy's home immediately because it was believed and feared that should that cock crow when the girl was still at home, refusing to follow the boy or making unnecessary preparations, she or somebody else in her family would instantly die.

Another type of oruhoko was done by smearing millet flour on the face of the girl. If the boy chanced to find the girl grinding millet, he would pick some flour from the winnowing tray used to collect the flour as it comes off the grinding stone and smear it on the girl's face. The boy would run away and swift arrangements would be made to send

him the girl as any delays and excuses would cause consequences similar to those associated with the other methods described above.

Among the Bahima especially, there were three other ways in which *okuteera oruhoko* would be done. One of them was for the boy to put a tethering rope around the neck of the girl and then pronounce in public that he had done so. The second one was to put a plant known as *orwihura* on the girl's head; and the third one was for the boy to sprinkle milk into the girl's face while milking. It should be pointed out that this practice was possible if the boy and the girl belonged to different clans.

Oruhoko was a dangerous and degrading practice. It was usually tried by boys who failed to have alternatives. If the boy was not lucky enough to elude and run faster than the relatives of the girl, he would be killed. It was, however, usually done so abruptly that before the girl's relatives could get organised, the boy would have disappeared. The punishment was usually inflicted on the boy through the payment of too much bridewealth. He would pay double the normal charge or even more. The extra cows which were charged were not refunded if the marriage broke up.

## Birth

The Banyankore did not have peculiar birth customs. Usually, when a woman was to give birth for the first time, she would be sent to her mother. Brave women, and the majority of them were brave, could give birth by themselves without any need for a midwife. However, if things went wrong, an acting midwife, usually an old woman would be summoned.

If the afterbirth refused to come out freely and quickly after the child, some medicine would be administered to the woman. If the normal herbs failed to induce it to come out, the husband of the woman was required to climb with a mortar to the top of the house, raise the alarm and slide the mortar down from the top of the house. It was believed that the afterbirth would come out as the mortar was sliding down from the top of the house.

## Naming

The child could be named immediately after birth. The normal practice was after the mother had finished the days of confinement referred to as *ekiriri*. The woman could confine herself for four days if the child was a boy and for three days if it was a girl. After three or four days, as the case may be, the couple would officially resume their sexual relationship in a practice known as *okucwa ekizaire*. The name given to a child depended on the personal experience of the father and the mother, the time when the child was born, the days of the week, the place of birth, or the name of an ancestor. The name could be given by the father, the grandfather or even the mother of the child. However, the father's choice usually took precedence.

The names given were verbs or nouns that could appear in normal speech. Often the names also portrayed the state of mind of the persons who gave them. For example, the name *Kaheeru* among the Banyoro portrayed the fact that the husband suspected that the woman had got the baby outside the family. In traditional Ankole, it was normal practice for a woman to have sex with her in-laws and even have children by them. Such children were not regarded any differently from the other children in the family.

## Death

The Banyankore did not believe that death was a natural phenomenon. According to them, death was attributed to sorcery, misfortune and the spite of the neighbours. They even had a saying: *"Tihariho mufu atarogyirwe"* meaning: "There is nobody who dies without being bewitched". They found it hard to believe that a man could die if it was not due to witchcraft and malevolence of other persons. Accordingly, after every death, the persons affected would consult a witch doctor to detect whoever was responsible for causing the death.

A dead body would normally stay in the house for as long as it would take all the important relatives to gather. Among the Bairu a person could be buried either in the compound or in the plantation. Among the Bahima he would be buried in the kraal. Burial was usually done in the afternoon and bodies were buried facing the east. A woman was made to lie on her left while a man was laid on his right. After burial, a woman was accorded three days of mourning while a man was accorded four days. During the days of mourning, all the neighbours and the relatives of the deceased would remain camping and sleeping at the home of the deceased. During this period, the whole neighbourhood would not dig or do manual work because it was believed that if anyone dug or did manual work during the mourning days, he would cause the whole village to be ravaged by hail storms. Such a person could also be regarded as a sorcerer and could easily be suspected of having caused the death of the person who had just been buried. However, the abstinence of the neighbours from digging and doing manual work was meant to console the relatives.

If the dead man was the head of the household, his leading bull would be killed and eaten to end the days of mourning. Further ritual ceremonies would be conducted if the dead man was very old and had grandchildren. If a person died with a grudge against someone in the family, he was buried with some objects to keep the spirit occupied so that it would fail to have time to haunt those with whom the deceased had a grudge.

There were special burials for spinsters and those who committed suicide. It was considered taboo for one to commit suicide. The burial of one who committed suicide was very complicated. The body would be cut from the tree by a woman who had attained menopause (*encurazaara*). Such a woman was heavily fortified with charms. Indeed it was believed that whoever performed the role of cutting the rope used by the suicide would soon die also.

Tradition has it that at times, the corpses of suicide victims could not be touched. A grave was dug directly under the corpse so that when cutting the rope, the corpse would fall into the grave. The grave was then covered and that was all. There would be neither mourning nor the normal funeral rites. The tree on which the victim had hanged himself would be uprooted and burnt. The relatives of the suicide victim would not use any piece of that tree for firewood.

There were also particular formalities for the burial of a spinster. If such a girl died, it was feared that her spirit would return to disturb the living simply because the girl had died unsatisfied. In order to placate the spirit and avert its evil retributions, before the body was taken for burial, one of the dead girl's brothers was required to pretend to be making love with the corpse. This act was known as *okugyeza empango ahamutwe*. Then the body was passed by the rear door and buried. It is said that if a man grew old and died unmarried, he would be buried with a banana stem to occupy the position of the supposed wife. This was believed to propitiate the dead man's spirit and its evil retributions on the living. The body was also passed through the rear door of the house.

## Blood brotherhood

The Banyankore had a practice of making blood brotherhood. A person would make a blood brother in a ceremony known as *okukora omukago*. The actual ceremony involved the two people sitting on a mat so close together that their legs would overlap. In their right hands, they would hold sprouts of *ejubwe* type of grass and a sprout of *omurinzi* tree (*erythina tomentosa*). The Bairu would hold in addition a sprout of *omutoma*   (fig) tree (*ficus eryobotrioides*).

The master of ceremonies would make a small cut to the right of the navel of each man. The end of the omurinzi tree and ejubwe grass were dipped in the blood on the incision and put into the hands of each person. For the Bahima, only the *mutoma* sprout was used. Then a little milk was poured in the blood or a little millet flour in the case of the Bairu and each man would hold the other's hand with the left and they would both swallow the blood and milk or the blood and millet flour in each other's hand at the same time.

Blood brotherhood could not be made between people of the same clan because naturally, they would be regarded as brothers. Blood brothers would treat each other as real brothers in every respect.

## Political set-up

The Banyankore had a centralised system of government. At the top of the political ladder there was the king called *Omugabe*. Below him there was the Prime Minister known as *Enganzi*. Then there were provincial chiefs known as *Abakuru b'ebyanga*. Below them, there were the chiefs who took charge of local affairs at the parish and sub-parish levels.

The position of the king was hereditary.

*Sir Charles Gasyonga, Omugabe of Ankole*

The king had to belong to the Bahinda royal clan who claimed descent from Ruhinda, son of *Njunaki*. Whenever a king died, there were often succession disputes to determine who would succeed to the throne. Thereafter, there would be an elaborate ceremony to install the new king. Whenever a king died, some of his wives would commit suicide or they would be forced to do so. Some of the servants in the royal court would also commit suicide. It is said that in earlier times, some people of the *Basingo* clan would also be killed in order to accompany the king in the afterworld. The corpse of the king was referred to as *omuguta* to distinguish it from that of an ordinary person which was known as *omurambo*. It was specially buried by the *Bayangwe* clan styling themselves for the occasion as the *Abahitsi*. To communicate the message that the king had died, one would not say that *Omugabe afiire* which is the appropriate Runyankore term, rather, one would say that *Omugabe ataahize*.

## Wars

The kingdom had a standing army. The army was divided into battalions known as *emitwe* (singular: *omutwe*). Each battalion was under a provincial head known as *Mukuru w'ekyanga* sometimes referred to as *Omukungu*. Often the kingdom of Nkore was at war with the neighbouring states and sometimes she sent raiding expeditions to Karagwe and Buhweju. The kingdom of Bunyoro sometimes raided Nkore and took away a lot of cattle. Notable among the Banyoro invasions of Nkore were those of Omukama Olimi I during the reign of Ntare I Nyabugaro and that of Omukama I Wamali in the 17th century during the reign of Ntare IV Kitabanyoro. During the reign of Ntare IV, there occurred another war between the Banyankore and the *Nkondami* (soldiers) of Kabundami of Buhweju.

During the reign of King Machwa after the death of Ntare IV, an expedition was sent against Irebe, the king of Bwera. The expedition brought a lot of plunder among which were cattle and Irebe's sacred circlet, *Rutare*, which was thereafter used by the Bagabe of Nkore in making rain. Another invasion of Nkore took place during the reign of Kahaya I Nyamwanga. This invasion was by the Banyarwanda under their king Kigyeri III Ndabarasa.

### The royal regalia

The royal regalia of Ankole consisted of a spear and drums. The main instrument of power was the royal drum called *Bagyendan-wa*. This drum was believed to have been made by Wamala, the last Muchwezi ruler. This drum was only beaten at the installation of a new king. It had its special hut and it was considered taboo to shut the hut. A fire was always kept burning for Bagyendanwa and this fire could only be extinguished in the event of the death of the king. The drum had its own cows and some other attendant drums

namely: *Kabembura, Nyakashaija, Eigura, Kooma* and *Njeru ya Buremba* which was obtained from the kingdom of Buzimba.

### Religion

The Banyankore's idea of a supreme being was *Ruhanga* (Creator). The abode of Ruhanga was said to be in heaven, just above the clouds. Ruhanga was believed to be the maker and giver of all things. It was, however, believed that evil persons could use black magic to interfere with the good wishes of Ruhanga and cause ill-health, drought, death or even barrenness in the land and among the people.

At a lower level, the idea of Ruhanga was expressed in the cult of *Emandwa*. These were gods particular to different families and clans and they were easily approachable in the event of need. Each family had a shrine where the family gods were supposed to dwell. Whenever beer was brewed or a goat slaughtered, a gourd full of beer and some small bits

*The royal drum* **Bagyendanwa** *with its consort* **Kabembura** (on the right) *and attendant drums. In front, the keeper of the drums, Mrs. Kicada of the Baruru clan*

*A Munyankore woman in traditional dress*

*A Munyankore man in traditional dress*

of meat were put in the shrine for the *mandwa*. In the event of sickness or misfortune, the family members would perform rituals called *okubandwa* as a way of supplicating the gods to avert sickness or misfortune.

## Entereko

The Banyankore brewed beer by squeezing ripe bananas and mixing the resulting juice with water and sorghum and then letting the mixture ferment overnight in a wooden trough called *obwato*. Beer was required at every social gathering be it a wedding, funeral, self-help communal work or any other function.

Whenever beer was made, the Banyankole had what they called *entereko*. If someone brewed beer, he had to reserve some for the neighbours as a sign of belonging and good neighbourliness. This beer so reserved was known as entereko.

Normally, one or two days after someone had brewed beer, he would call his neighbours and serve them the reserved beer. This practice was so important that anyone who failed to comply with it was considered a bad neighbour. He would not be accorded the services of the neighbours in the event of need.

During the service of the entereko, the men would discuss important matters of substance that affected their area in particular, the kingdom and beyond. There would be a lot of merrymaking including dancing. The traditional dance among the Banyankore was called *ekyitaguriro* and men and women would participate in it. The Bahima also sang and

**(Above):** Ekitaguriro: *traditional Ankole dance.*    **(Below):** *Banyankore men blend tradition with modernity,wrapping* bikohe *around their trousers.*

*Making beer from bananas in Ankole*

made competitive recitals connected with valour in wars of offence and defence and about cattle.

The staple food of the Banyankore was millet. It was supplemented with bananas, potatoes and cassava. A rich and prosperous family was judged by its ability to maintain food supplies throughout the year. The main sauces were beans, peas, and groundnuts plus a variety of greens such as *eshwiga, enyabutongo, dodo, ekyijamba, omugobe, omuriri* and some others as well as meat of both domestic and wild animals.

A family that could not produce or store enough food to sustain itself for most of the year was not respected. In times of shortages, a woman and her daughters would go and work for food by digging in another family's garden. This practice was called *okushaka*. It was very degrading and brought shame on the family concerned. In fact it would result in the daughters of that family failing to attract would-be suitors because it would be well

known in the area that they belonged to a lazy home.

Millet and meat were prepared for important occasions. Potatoes and cassava were not respectable foods and unless there was a real shortage of food, they could not be presented to a visitor or be eaten for the evening meal. Leftovers were common and could be eaten. It was rare for a family to eat and finish a whole meal. However, the family head was not supposed to eat leftovers. Besides, men and boys were advised not to eat a burnt potato. The reason was that it was so sweet that if ever the man remembered its sweetness while away on a hunt or at work, he might be tempted to leave his duties and come home. Such food was eaten by women and children. The main food of the Bahima was milk and baked blood called *enjuba*. They would, in addition barter potatoes, cassava and *matoke* from the agriculturalists in exchange for milk and ghee. In times of real scarcity, the Bahima could just subsist on milk and blood.

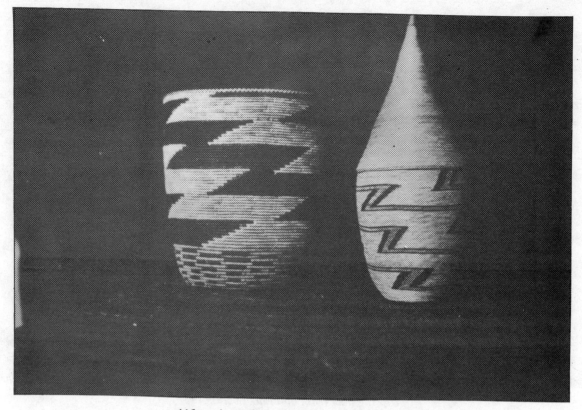

(Above): *Ankole baskets*
(Below): *Ekyanzi: a decorated Ankole milk pot*

## Method of counting

The Banyankore had their own method of counting. They could count from one to ten using fingers. One was indicated by showing only the forefinger. Two was indicated by showing the first and second fingers; three was indicated by raising the last three fingers; four was indicated by snapping the first and the third fingers of one's hand, and five was counted by clenching the fist with the thumb enclosed. Six was indicated by showing the first, second and third fingers. Seven was implied by holding down the third finger and showing the first, middle and last fingers. Eight was implied by snapping the first fingers of both hands; nine was indicated by clenching the middle finger with the thumb; and clenching the fist with the thumb outside meant ten.

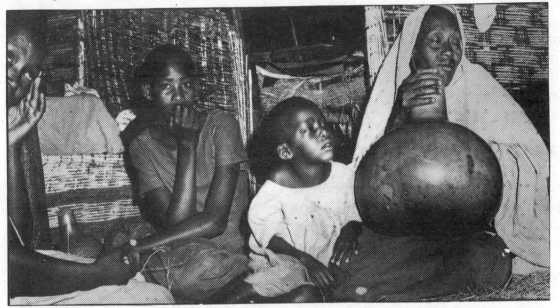

(Above): *Inside a Hima hut* (Below): *A Munyankore making fire by rubbing sticks* (oburindi)

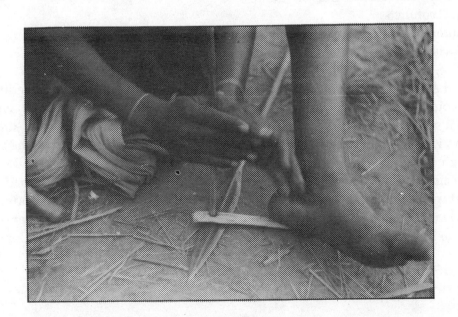

# The Bakiga

The Bakiga inhabit Kabale and part of Rukungiri districts. They occupy the counties of Ndorwa, Rubanda, Rukiga in Kabale and parts of Kinkizi and Rubabo counties in Rukungiri district. Due to overpopulation, the Bakiga have been migrating to other parts of Uganda especially to Kabarole, Rukungiri, Kasese, Hoima, Masindi and Mubende districts; and Rwampara, Ruhama and Ibanda counties of Mbarara district. They have also settled in Masaka and Rakai districts. They are a physically strong people. They speak *Rukiga*, a Bantu language.

## Origins

The actual origins of the Bakiga are hidden in varying traditions. Some say that the Bakiga originally lived in Karagwe having migrated from Bunyoro during the Luo invasion. They are associated with the Banyambo of Tanzania. Another tradition which seems more sensible says that the cradle of the Bakiga was in Buganza in Rwanda. They migrated from Buganza in search of fertile land and to escape natural hazards or due to internal political conflicts.

From Rwanda, the Bakiga are said to have migrated to Bwisa, to Bugoyi, then to Rutchuru, all in Zaire, and they finally settled in Kigezi. Since the Bakiga are Bantu speakers, this tradition could be true. What may equally be true is that the Bakiga were part of the Bantu speakers who migrated from the Congo region, through Bunyoro, Karagwe, Rwanda and eastern Zaire to finally settle in Kigezi. What has not yet been established are the exact dates when they settled in each of the areas en route to Kigezi.

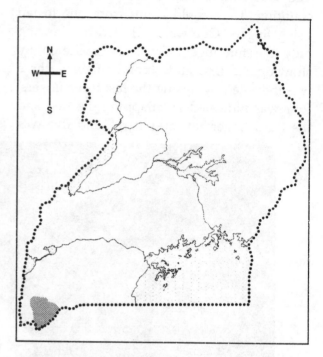

## Social set-up

The Bakiga were organised into clans the biggest of which was the Basigi clan. Each clan was composed of several lineages and each lineage had a head, *Omukuru w'omuryango*. A man was not allowed to marry from his clan.

## Marriage

Marriage was a very important cultural institution among the Bakiga. Traditionally, no marriage could be honoured without the payment of bridewealth. In the past a marriage could be arranged by the boy's father or uncle on the boy's behalf. The final arrangements could only be made after the payment of bridewealth. The bridewealth was normally paid by the boy's father. It involved cows, goats and hoes. The amount paid

*Bakiga hunters in typical Kigezi countryside*

differed from group to group and from family to family within each group. It is said that it was taboo to sell any animals given as bridewealth. Such animals could be used to obtain wives for the girl's brothers or father. The Bakiga are a very polygamous society; the number of wives was only limited by the availability of land and bridewealth obligations.

The bridewealth paid on a girl was shared among the girl's principal relatives. Of the relatives the most important were *Nyinarimi* (maternal uncle) and *Ishenkazi* (paternal aunt). If one of them went away dissatisfied, so they said, he could render the girl barren or cause her to have incessant ill-health by inciting the wrath of the ancestors.

Boys tended to marry at a slightly late age, between eighteen and twenty years, while girls could be married off between fourteen and sixteen years of age. The normal trend was for girls from richer families to get married later than girls from poorer families. Before marriage, a girl would spend a month or so in seclusion. During this period, she would be well fed and instructed in the art of home management.

## Divorce

Divorce was a common phenomenon among the Bakiga. The common causes were barrenness and laziness on the part of the wife or the husband. Some other matters of misunderstanding between a husband and a wife could also lead to divorce. A divorcee was allowed to remarry but she would fetch less bridewealth this time as she would no longer be a virgin. The majority of the would-be instances of divorce were settled by the elders. They would normally be called by the woman's father to listen to both the husband and the wife and try to have the two sides reach an amicable conclusion that would

*A Mukiga mother transporting food*

prevent divorce. In such cases it was normal to fine the offending party. Fighting in the home between husbands and wives was frequent, but it would not normally lead to divorce.

## Religion

The Bakiga believed in a supreme being, *Ruhanga*, the Creator of all things earthly and heavenly. At a lower level, they believed in the cult of *Nyabingi*. The Nyabingi cult was said to have originated from Karagwe. It had its base at Kagarama, near Lake Bunyonyi. There were special shrines for Nyabingi known as *endaro*. Through Nyabingi's representatives known as *Abagirwa* people would worship and tender sacrifices of beer and roasted meat to Nyabingi.

## Economy

The Bakiga were basically agriculturalists growing mainly sorghum, peas, millet and beans. They also reared some cattle, sheep and goats. Among them were excellent iron-smiths who made hoes, knives and spears. They were also great potters and produced a wide assortment of pottery. Besides, they made a wide range of carpentry object baskets and mats and they reared bees and produced honey.

The Bakiga lived and worked communally. Most economic activities were done on a communal basis. Grazing, bush clearing, cultivation and harvesting were done communally. The men cleared the bush while the women tilled the land. Men worked together to erect round, grass-thatched huts for shelter. They practised barter trade amongst themselves and between their neighbours.

The staple foods of the Bakiga were sorghum, beans and peas. They supplemented them with pumpkins, yams, meat and a variety of green vegetables. Sufficient food was prepared so that everyone could eat his fill. It was considered good manners to join in whenever one found a given family at a meal. One would just wash one's hands and join the others without waiting to be invited. If a man had more than one wife, all his women had to serve him at each meal. He could eat the most delicious share of the food among the lot, or all of it if he so wished.

The Bakiga made beer from sorghum. The beer, *omuramba*, played a significant social role. It had a food component and was an alcoholic drink necessary for social gatherings. Omuramba was normally taken from a pot placed in a convenient place. The men would sit on wooden stools surrounding it and by means of long tubes, they would drink as they discussed matters affecting their country. The elders would also settle disputes, recite their heroic deeds and their history, and sing and dance around a pot of omuramba.

The Bakiga were and still are very good zither (*enanga*) players. They played it alone or in groups.

## Utensils

The Bakiga's domestic utensils included baskets, pots, winnowing trays, stools, grinding stones, wooden pestles, mortars and mingling ladles. The other household items were drums and harps for entertainment; spears, bows and arrows for defence and hunting; grass mats (*ebirago*) for sleeping on and *emishambi* for sitting on. Previously the Bakiga women dressed in cow hides known as *ebishato* or *enkanda*. They wore bangles on their legs and arms.

## Political set-up

The Bakiga were a segmentary society. Political authority rested in the hands of the lineage

*A traditional dance of the Bakiga*

*A traditional homestead of the Bakiga with sorghum stores*

leaders, *Abakuru b'emiryango*, many of whom had excellent oratory as well as military skills. They were supposed to be impartial in administering justice. Some leaders such as *Basubi* emerged to prominence because they had mystical skills. They were rainmakers. Others were *Bagirwa*, the mediums of the *Nyabingi* cult.

The Bakiga were warlike. They resisted the *Batutsi* and *Bahima* incursions. As a politically segmented society, they did not have a standing army. However, they had warlords who would mobilise and lead the people to war in the event of invasion. The warlords were men who had killed a large number of enemies in wars without losing any of their men or weapons. Every able-bodied male was culturally obliged to be a soldier.

## Judicial system

The Bakiga abhorred anti-social activities and if any one was caught he was heavily punished. Such activities included stealing, blocking paths, murder, sorcery and night dancing. In the case of murder, for example, the murderer was buried alive in the same grave as his victim. Virginity was highly esteemed and it was a very serious offence for a girl to get pregnant before marriage. If an unmarried girl became pregnant, she would either be taken to a forest and be tied to a tree and left for wild animals or, she would be tied feet and arms and thrown over a cliff. Most pregnant girls among the Bakiga were taken to the Kisizi falls in Ndorwa and thrown down the cliff. They would drown in the falls. The lucky ones were simply cursed and disowned by their people.

# The Banyarwanda/Bafumbira

The Banyarwanda or Bafumbira are found in the old districts of Ankole and Kigezi bordering Rwanda. They have, however, spread to many parts of Uganda. Ethnically, they are the same as the Banyarwanda of Rwanda. Those who inhabit Kisoro District in the extreme southwest of Uganda, are called Bafumbira. This is the only district that is inhabited almost exclusively by Banyarwanda. To their west, is Zaire and to their south is Rwanda. Their land is mountainous and cool. Bufumbira was part of Rwanda until the boundary adjustments of 1910. The actual inhabitants of Bufumbira, in descending order of numerical superiority, are the *Bahutu*, the *Batutsi* and the *Batwa*. Essentially, they are Banyarwanda and they speak Kinyarwanda.

The Batwa are said to have been the original inhabitants of Bufumbira and they are closely related to the Bambuti of Mt. Rwenzori. The Bahutu are said to have been the second group to arrive in Bufumbira. Then came the Batutsi before A.D.1500.

## Origins

The Batwa do not have traditions of early migration from anywhere. They are believed to have been the earliest inhabitants of East Africa together with the Bambuti of Mt. Rwenzori and the Ndorobo of Kenya. To date they do not lead a permanent, settled life. The Bahutu are Bantu and, like other Bantu, they are believed to have originated from the Congo region of Central Africa around A.D1000. They are said to have entered Rwanda from the northeast.

The origin of the Batutsi is, however, mythical. One theory says that they originated from Karagwe in northern Tanzania. Another very controversial one is the "Hamitic myth".

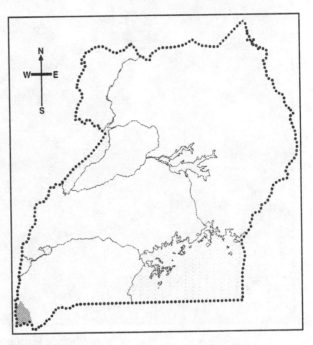

This theory has it that the Batutsi are not indigenous to East Africa. And that their original homeland might have been either Somalia or Ethiopia or Egypt. This theory is based, among other things, on the fact that the Batutsi tend to resemble the Somali and the Galla.

## Social set-up

The Batwa were a minority in Bufumbira and in other Banyarwanda communities. They were the most scorned, mainly because their culture was very little understood. It is said that no one ever saw a Mutwa's grave; no one knew when and how the Batwa organised their wedding ceremonies. Their incessant begging from the Bahutu and Batutsi increased the scorn and disrespect directed at the Batwa. Those Batwa who lived in and around Chunya Bamboo Forest Reserve were experts at shooting with bows and arrows. They lived by hunting and gathering, eating

*A Mutwa man playing a* nanga

not only what they hunted and gathered but also what Bahutu and the Batutsi neglected. They were also reputed mutton eaters.

The cultures of the Bahutu and Batutsi were similar. Like the majority of the Bahutu, the Batutsi did not eat sheep and chicken. These, they gave to the Batwa. Besides, the Bahutu and Batutsi women were not supposed to eat goat meat.

## Marriage

Compared to the Batwa and the Bahutu, the Batutsi married at a later age. Although there seemed to be no taboos against marriage relationships, intermarriages between the Batwa, Bahutu and the Batutsi were rare.

Among the Bahutu and the Batutsi, inter-marriages between close relatives were prohibited on the claim that this connection would render the resulting offspring weak and vulnerable to spiritual attacks. Among the

Batutsi, boys were usually pressed to marry even before they were ready. The girls were closely watched by their mothers and aunts. Virginity was highly prized. Premarital preg-nancies were unwanted. A girl would be thrown into a forest and left to the mercy of wild animals if she conceived before marriage.

Formerly, parents would arrange marriages for their children. But there was also what was known as *gufata* or *gaturura*. Gufata was an acceptable forced-marriage in which a boy would conspire to and carry away a girl by force to become his wife. Among the Bahutu, there was also what was known as *ukwijana*. This was a pre-arranged marriage in which the girl would sneak away from her parents and go to a boy's home to get married. This occurred whenever a girl had a pre-marital pregnancy. Both gufata and ukwijana were socially accepted but not praiseworthy.

Bridewealth was paid in the form of cows and goats. If a girl was forced into marriage, exorbitant bridewealth was paid. On the other hand, if a girl went to the boy's home to get married, the bridewealth depended on how the girl went there. If it was the girl who decided to go, the bridewealth would be small, but if it was the boy who wooed, it would be exorbitant. Thereafter, wedding arrangements would be entered into. On the wedding day, local sorghum beer and banana beer were served. The wedding day was called *ubukwe* or *ubushyitsi*. On that day the bride would be carried to the bridegroom's home on a litter. The wedding celebrations took place at night and carried on into the morning hours.

On wedding days, traditional dances were performed. The women would ululate while men sang and recited great historical events. They danced in pairs. The men would also jump. The musical instruments were drums and harps. Clapping was a common feature for all the groups. The Batwa were renowned harp players while the Bahutu, like the Bakiga, played the zither. Among the Batutsi, the girls sang and danced in pairs while men danced in groups usually of more than ten people, called *intore*.

Polygamy was an acceptable practice. Not only did it increase the man's status, but it also increased the family size. "Being monogamous was like marrying one's mother", so they said. Divorce was also acceptable and could occur in any of the following instances: drunkenness, ill-treatment, adultery, gluttony, refusal or inability to offer sex, and several other socially undesirable instances.

## Economy

The economy of the Batwa was quite simple. They depended on hunting and gathering. They valued land least for they did not dig. They would get grains and beer from the Bahutu and the Batutsi in exchange for wild animal skins, trophies, bows and arrows. Some Batwa would just live by begging. Their huts were as simple as those of the Bambuti. They used to wear a simple skin to cover their private parts. Batwa were, and continue to be, good at basketry and pottery.

Among the Bahutu and the Batutsi, the ownership of a Mutwa was a sign of wealth and security. Among the Bahutu and the Batutsi, cattle was the main economic index. For this reason, the Batutsi were most respected because they had many herds of cattle. People did not have individual owner-

*Banyarwanda* intore *dancers*

*A Munyarwanda potter making a clay pot*

ship of land because all the land belonged to the king. An individual could dig or graze cattle on any piece of land within reach of his home.

For digging, they used a hooked wooden hoe. The main crops included sorghum, peas and beans. The society had iron-smiths who manufactured hoes, knives and other implements on a small scale. To harvest sorghum, they used a sickle, *umuhoro*. Men cut the sorghum down and women used iron knives, *indiga*, to cut the sorghum from the stems. The produce was stored in bamboo granaries constructed in the compound.

Bahutu were good brewers. They brewed beer from sorghum. The local brew had various names: *umuramba, wutunda, nyirakabisi* and *amarwa*. If it was mixed with honey, it would be referred to as *inturire*. Inturire was a brew for elders and chiefs. The women were not allowed to drink in public. In fact their preserve was the dregs. The elders smoked pipes containing unprocessed tobacco. The Batwa could, in addition to tobacco, smoke opium.

## Dwellings

The Bahutu and the Batutsi lived in homesteads. The exact structure of their hut was round, grass-thatched and white sand-washed. Unlike the Batwa, the duty of constructing and maintaining huts among the Bahutu and the Batutsi was entrusted to men. All the families were extended and patrilineal. Single clans tended to live together in one locality.

## Sports and personal adornments

The most favoured sport among the Bafumbira was hunting. When hunting they used dogs with bells tied around their necks, hunting nets, spears, clubs and bows, and

*Banyarwanda war dance*

arrows. The other favoured sports were wrestling, jumping and a mweso board game, especially among the Batutsi. It was known as *igisoro*.

The Bahutu branded their faces using very small, hot, iron knives. This was done as a way of treating headaches. The Batutsi put one small mark on their faces for purposes of identification. The Batwa went further than other groups to the extent of decorating their arms. Neck beads and bangles were common adornments for women.

## Religion

The Bahutu and the Batutsi believed in a supreme being called *Imana* or *Rurema*. Imana was believed to be the Creator and giver of all things and was believed to have mediums in the form of either *Nyabingi* or *Lyangombe Biheko*. Sacrifices were offered to Nyabingi and Biheko and each family had a shrine, indaro. Indaro was regarded as a very sacred place and the family head would offer sorghum; bread and beer to the gods as circumstances

*Batutsi men in Bufumbira*

indicated. If the head of the family died, his first-born or first son would take over all the duties of tendering sacrifices to the gods in the family *indaro*.

## Burial

The Bahutu and the Batutsi bury their dead. For anybody above eighteen years of age, there would be four days of mourning. During the time of mourning, there would be no digging or any kind of manual labour. During the dawn of the fourth day, a special ceremony known as *Guta igiti* (throwing off the ash) was conducted by a skilled medicine man; and the heir to the deceased, where appropriate, was installed. In case the deceased was an old man with daughters-in-law, the wife of the eldest son would dress the corpse and she would be given one of the deceased's gardens for this task.

## Utensils

The traditional household utensils included baskets, winnowing trays, grinding stones, an assortment of pottery products, calabashes, gourds, mortars and pestles, *imitiba* (huge bamboo store baskets inside the house), wooden stools, spears, knives, bows and arrows. Cattle keepers kept, in addition, *inkongoro* for milking cows and *ibisabo* (churning gourds) and other milk containers. The inner rooms were kept covered by nicely decorated mats made of swamp grass and embroidered with strings. These mats made favourite seats for women during wedding ceremonies and feasts. One could also find huge mats known as *ibirago* used for drying sorghum and other produce.

## Political set-up

The Batutsi aristocrats were the traditional rulers over their fellow Batutsi, the Bahutu and the Batwa communities. Leadership was hereditary. The head of government was the king, *Umwami*. He was assisted by the land (*Umunyabutaka*) and cattle or grass (*Umunyamukenke*) chiefs. The land chief was in turn assisted by subordinate chiefs known as *Ibisonga* and *Abakoresha*. The king had a standing army (*Intore*) which consisted of professional Batutsi, Bahutu and Batwa warriors.

There was a clientele system known as *ubuhake* whereby a Muhutu, upon being given a cow, would render clientage, bordering on servitude, to a Mututsi. To cement community relations, a system of blood brotherhood was practised. It consisted of sucking one another's blood from the navel and taking an oath to treat each other as real brothers. The contracting parties would then offer gifts to each other.

## Judicial system

Thieves and wizards were highly decried. They would be speared or beaten to death whenever they were caught. A woman who poisoned a person to death, would also be given poison to drink. Normally, the family heads and elders would settle civil and criminal cases. Female fighting was decried but male fighting was treated lightly. The common saying was that "those who fight are they that have their stomachs full".

Whenever there was a fight in a family and it ended in a divorce, the case would appear before the elders. If the husband was proved guilty, he would offer a pot of beer and a goat to the woman's family and redeem his wife. If it was the woman who was found guilty, she was verbally disciplined. No fine was levied on a woman for fear that it might cause trouble in the family.

# The Basoga

The Basoga are the eastern neighbours of the Baganda. They occupy the region between Lake Victoria and Lake Kioga in the present districts of Jinja, Kamuli and Iganga.

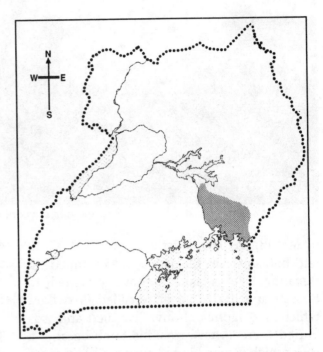

## Origin

Due to the continuous movements and intermingling of people within the Basoga region, the history of the Basoga is complex. It can be asserted, however, that the earliest inhabitants of Busoga belonged to the same Bantu group comprising the Banyoro and the Baganda. Their origins can therefore be traced, like other Bantu groups, to the Katanga region of Central Africa.

Tradition holds that the earliest inhabitants were the Langi, the Iteso and the Bagisu. They were later engulfed by migrants from Buganda.

The earliest settlers in Busoga are said to have occupied the lake-shore areas of modern Bukoli. Nanyumba's Banyole are believed to have been among these earliest inhabitants. These early settlements took place far back in the 14th century. They were later joined by other people from the Mt. Elgon region. These people are said to have been led by Kintu and are said to have settled in Bugabula and Bulamogi. They were later joined by others from Budama and some from Kigulu in Kenya.

## Legend

There are three legends regarding the origins of the Basoga. One of them talks of the famous hunter, Mukama, who came from the East side of Mt. Elgon and crossed into Busoga via present Bugisu and Budama. He is said to have been accompanied by his wives, various followers and two dogs.

Mukama had eight sons during his stay in Busoga. These sons were subsequently appointed rulers over certain areas. Mukama proceeded to Bunyoro where he set up a kingdom. He died of smallpox in Bunyoro and that is why the relatives of Mukama in Busoga do not look at a patient suffering from smallpox. It is also customary that no member of the Ngobi clan passes by another one suffering from smallpox without touching him.

The second legend insists that Mukama did not come to Busoga at all that Mukama only sent his own sons to rule Busoga because there were no capable rulers among the Basoga.

The third legend talks of Kintu as having been the man called Mukama and it was this same Kintu who came to Busoga from the east

*Basoga musicians playing amadinda*

of Mt. Elgon. This legend asserts that Kintu left his sons in Busoga and continued to Buganda. He is said to have returned to Busoga and lived in a place called Buswikira which is at Igombe, Bunya. He died and was buried there. Afterwards, his tomb became a rock which is worshipped even today by some Basoga.

Originally, the Basoga were a disunited people. They could not unite even in the face of a common enemy. This explains why they were incessantly prone to foreign influence first from Bunyoro and later from Buganda.

## Language

Lusoga language closely approximates to Luganda, especially that spoken by the Ssesse Islanders. There exist many Lusoga dialects. However Buganda influence over Busoga was so much that Luganda tends to be used as a lingua franca in Busoga more than Lusoga itself. Within Busoga, there are so many dialects of the Lusoga language that it is difficult to reach agreement on the correct way to spell or pronounce certain words. For instance, in the north of Busoga, there is a distinct *H* but people from southern Busoga

do not accept this *H* as being appropriate to the Lusoga Language.

## Luo influences

The Basoga were also under the influence of the Luo rulers of Bunyoro. As a result, the Basoga followed some of the Luo customs. For example, at puberty, they used to extract the six teeth in the lower jaw as an initiation to adulthood like the Alur of West Nile and the Joluo of western Kenya. Even some of their ceremonies, especially those regarding death, tended to resemble those of the Luo.

## Land ownership and the economy

In Busoga, each clan had land and the *Mutaka* (clan-head) was responsible for the clan's land. This land could not pass from the ownership of one clan to another nor could a member who was granted land by the clan-head be deprived of it. There was plenty of land in spite of the large population. Any member could get land by simply asking the clan-head for it.

A non-clan member could be allowed to cultivate land but only as a *Mugiha* (tenant).

The land could be taken from him should it be required by any member of the clan to which it belonged. They were settled agriculturalists and they were quite rich in food and cattle.

# Death and burial rites

## A chief

Whenever an important chief was sick, very few people were allowed to come near him. His death was first kept secret until all his wives, cattle, hoes, ivory, and male slaves had been secured. Thereafter, the official announcement was made early in the morning by a *Mujwa* (funeral official). It was then that the chief's wives, headmen, and people wept and kissed the corpse. No work of any kind could be done, not even visiting or cooking any kind of food. If there happened to be any other dead people, their burials had to wait until the chief's funeral rites were completed.

It was taboo for any cock to crow during that period. No one shaved until the rites were over. The older wives of the chief were gathered and kept in the death hut for seven days supporting the body of the dead chief across their feet. For these seven days, they were not supposed to touch food of any kind.

## Burial

The chief was buried in the hut of his first wife. He was buried with some objects, his body facing towards their supposed direction of origin. Most Basoga bury their dead facing northwards because they believe that they came from Bunyoro. The chief's grave was deep indeed, about ten metres.

Before burial, the corpse was washed all over by the wives. A new barkcloth was hung across the doorway of the hut. The corpse was smeared with butter and a large coloured bead was tied round the neck. In Bugabula, a piece of flayed cowhide was taken from a cow sacrificed to the dead and laid upon the forehead of the corpse. Other presents like beads, wires or bracelets were also put on the arms and legs of the corpse. The body was then carried to the burial hut by the *Bagwa* and put in the grave but no earth was put in yet. A bullock was tied to the doorway of the hut and dedicated to the dead chief. This ceremony was extended to inaugurate an heir.

## Burial of the head of family

All children kissed the corpse and wailed loudly. No cooking was allowed for one day. His grave could be dug in his own hut, garden or courtyard. The heir could be appointed at the time of burial. The other rites were like those of a chief but his grave was not reopened to add fresh barkcloths like the chief's. They could only sprinkle beer and blood over the grave.

## Burial of a childless man

A young man was treated like an old man. If he was unmarried, a widower, or married but without children, a broom was placed on the grave and he was ordered not to come back in the following words: "Go straight away and never return to earth, you childless one". His name was despised in the society and care was taken not to give it to another person for fear that he also might become childless.

## Burial of a married woman

The husband would wail and kiss the corpse and so would some relatives. She was buried in the banana plantation according to the customs of her husband. Often she was made to lie on her left. She was informed upon being buried that none of those present had caused her death and was implored not to come back for revenge.

Should she have possessed property, her spirit was placated by the offer of a goat or a bullock before the heir took over the property. Custom demanded that the dead woman's relatives should bring forward an unmarried girl and give her to the dead woman's husband. This girl became the heiress and took over the functions and property of the dead woman.

If the deceased woman had daughters who were married, their husbands had to redeem them from the death spirit with a goat. There was another special ceremony for a dead woman who left married sons. Each of the wives of her sons cooked food and took it to the place of burial where they would find their husband awaiting them.

The women dressed themselves up like men and went to the banana plantation. They would sit down in the manner men did when they went to arrange bridewealth or to redeem their wives from funeral rites. Their husbands would dress up like women and come to greet their wives. Then they would do all they could to make their wives laugh. If any of the women laughed, she was deemed unfit; the food she brought was considered unfit for

eating; and her marriage was cancelled.

In the case of a childless woman, the speaker said, "Never come back for you left nothing behind". A broom was then placed upon the grave and her name was allowed to die out of the society. Unmarried girls were buried in almost the same way as women, only no heiress was **necessary**.

*Basoga mukama fetish*

## Religion

The Basoga believed in the existence of a spirit world. They called the supreme being *Lubaale*. Human agents worked as messengers of Lubaale, or the ancestors, or other minor gods. To the Basoga, the spirit world, places of worship, animated objects and fetishes had power to do good or evil to the living. The Basoga call magicians, fetishmen and spirit mediums *Bacwezi*.

The Basoga believed in the existence of several gods and sub-gods. Below Lubaale, there was *Mukama*, the creator of all things; *Jingo*, the public god who attended to the general needs of the people; *Nawandyo*; and *Bilungo* the god of plagues. *Semaganda, Gasani* and *Kitaka* were other gods the Basoga believed in.

*Basoga fetish pot*

(Above): *Basoga girls dancing*
(Below): *Basoga flute players*

## Political set-up

There was no paramount chief over the whole of Basoga. The Basoga were organised into principalities or chiefdoms under the sovereignty of Bunyoro and later of Buganda. In the early times, the death of a chief was first reported to the Mukama of Bunyoro who would send the funeral barkcloth and all the necessary requirements for the burial rites. On several occasions, he used to appoint the heir or send back the son of the deceased chief if the son happened, as was usually the case, to be at the Mukama's court in Bunyoro.

During the time of the Luo migrations, Luo sub-dynasties were established in Busoga. Among these sub-dynasties (at least six in all), Bukoli and Bugwere were founded about the same time as the Babiito dynasty of Bunyoro at the beginning of the 16th century. By the turn of the 19th century, there were fifteen virtually independent principalities. In fact, the southern principalities are said to have been ruled by dynasties whose origins could be traced to the east and Lake Victoria Islands. During the 19th century, Buganda influence very greatly increased over the southern Busoga principalities. The northern principalities still had a connection with Bunyoro and indeed their language contained many Runyoro words.

In 1906 the British protectorate accomplished an administrative amalgamation of the multifarious kingdoms of pre-colonial Busoga into a single integrated structure. Representatives from the small pre-colonial kingdoms constituted the Busoga Lukiiko. In the same year Semei Kakungulu was appointed President of the Lukiiko, his reign ended with his resignation in 1913. This led to the collapse of the monstrous political structure and the abolition of the office of "President of the Lukiiko of Busoga". Later, there arose demands within Busoga for the revival of the office. In 1919 the Isebantu Kyabazinga office was established as an alternative to it. And Ezekieri Wako was appointed the first Isebantu Kyabazinga.

*Wilberforce K. Nandiope, the Kyabazinga of Busoga up to 1967*

# The Basamia-Bagwe

The Basamia-Bagwe are among the various ethnic groups that inhabit eastern Uganda. They can be traced in Tororo and Iganga districts. Some Basamia clans claim connection to the Joluo of Kenya while the Bagwe claim that they are related with the Banyala. This is further evidenced by the direction in which they face their dead during burial. Many Basamia clans face their dead to the southeast while the Bagwe face their dead to the east.

## Birth

In normal births, the mother confined herself for three days if the child was a boy and four days if the child was a girl. The birth of a boy was accorded fewer days of confinement to symbolise the fact that a man should get up very early to go and fight or do his own work. As for a woman, she could take her time. However, the *Balundu* clan reversed this order. For the birth of a girls the mother confined herself for three days while for a boy, she confined herself for four days. Normally in all cases, after the child has been born, the mother and father shave their hair.

## Twins

In the event of the birth of twins, a sheep was slain by treading on it until it died. Every one present was supposed to participate in treading on this sheep. The purpose was to wash off any taboos that were known to accompany the birth of twins and cleanse the children.

The father of the twins or his brother would then go with a spear or a knife to the in-laws who would come with porridge in a calabash. A special calabash (or pot) with two openings was provided and the leading person would

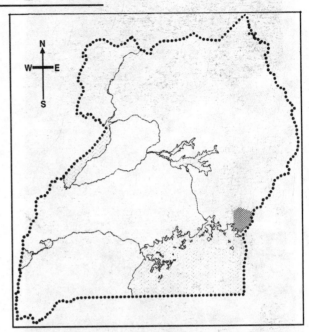

spit in it and then spit on the twins. This was done after having forced open the door of the hut in which the twins were with *olubibo* (forked sticks). During this ritual of opening the door, people would be dancing and singing obscene songs. After the door had been forced open, both the people inside and outside the hut would spit porridge on each other.

## Naming

Among the Basamia-Bagwe, naming was done immediately after the child had been born. Names were usually given by the mother depending on the circumstances under which the child had been born. Some of them were ordinary verbs that could be encountered in everyday speech, e.g. Wabwire (boy) or Nabwire (girl ) was given to a child who was born at night. Ojiambo or Ajiambo meant the child was born in the afternoon; Egesa or Nekesa meant the child was born during harvest.

*A Mugwe woman with decorations*

## Marriage

If the parents of the boy and the girl were friendly they could arrange the marriage without the boy and the girl being actively involved. But cases of this nature were rare. The usual method was that the boy would seduce the girl first. The girl could not show a concrete response although her response might appear positive. Thereafter, the boy would come with a spear and plant it in front of the hut of the girl's mother. If the girl had consented to marriage, she would remove the spear and take it inside her mother's hut. Thereafter bridewealth negotiations would be entered into.

There was no fixed bridewealth for each girl. One was charged depending on one's status, wealth and titles. This meant in effect, that the rich were charged more than the poor.

The general price ranged from between four and eight cows plus a large assortment of goats each of which had a specific role. Upon the payment of the bridewealth, further arrangements were made to take the girl to her husband. If it was discovered that the girl was a virgin, a goat or its equivalent would be sent to the girl's mother as a sign of appreciation for the good role she had played in keeping the girl intact and safe.

It was also customary for the boy to take a fat male goat to be slaughtered at the girl's father's home. This goat was known as *esidiso*. On this occasion, the girl's father would stand on it and be smeared with simsim oil. This male goat was meant to cement the marriage and it acted, in addition, as a common bond between the two families.

## Religion and taboos

The Basamia-Bagwe had an idea of a supreme being called *Were* or *Nasaye*. Were was said to dwell in heaven and to be responsible for creating the earth and the heavenly bodies. They also believed in ancestral spirits. Ancestral spirits were believed to intervene in human affairs and were known to cause harm, death and misfortune if not properly attended to. For this reason, each homestead had a family shrine on which to feed and appease the ancestral spirits. These spirits could be called upon in the event of sickness or misfortune and they were normally appealed to for good health, fertility of women and good harvests.

The Basamia-Bagwe believed in the existence of *omwoyo*, the heart of a living thing. They believed that when someone died, then omwoyo would take flight in the form of a shadow or wind. Such a departed spirit becomes *omusambwa*. It resides in graveyards and shrines.

*Emisambwa* are believed to have power to interfere with the living. They also act as a link

*A depiction of omusambwa in Samia-Bugwe*

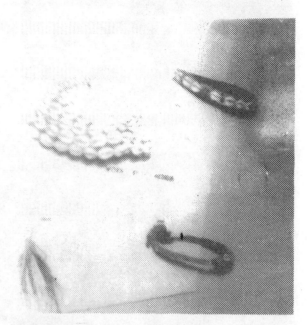

*A fetish dress for* emisambwa *worship (Samia-Bugwe)*

between *Nasaye* and the living. Emisambwa had their abode in *Emagombe*, i.e. in the underworld. Their taboos varied from clan to clan and no one would eat his totem. The society was patrilineal and women took up the clans and taboos of their husbands. It was taboo for a parent to sleep in the same hut as his son-in-law and once children had grown to a certain age, roughly ten years, they would not sleep in the same house as their parents. Women were not supposed to eat chicken, pork and lung-fish. The Basamia-Bagwe also believed in witchcraft and curses. Theft and immorality would result in being bewitched or cursed. Basamia-Bagwe also valued rainmakers, *abakimba*.

## Dress and food

The men used to wear goat-skins while women wore sketchy coverings made of tree leaves. The children walked around completely naked. The people used to sleep on a bare floor by a fire. If, however, someone was rich enough to afford it, he could sleep on a skin.

The staple foods were millet, sorghum and cassava. Women and girls ate together from the same plate while boys and their fathers would also eat together. Unnecessary talking was not allowed during normal eating and it was considered good manners to accept the offer when invited to eat.

## Political set-up

The political set-up of the Basamia-Bagwe was loose and segmentary. They did not have chieftainships. Every village was under the jurisdiction of an elder called the *Nalundiho*. Besides being a political figure, the Nalundiho was also a rainmaker. He administered law and order and he was responsible for settlement of disputes. He was the most influential person in the village and his position was hereditary. His powers were widened by his role as a rainmaker. It is said, for instance that if any one refused to settle his debt, the Nalundiho would deny that debtor's location rain until the debts were

*A Mugwe rainmaker from Masaba*

duly settled. Because of his capacity as a rainmaker, nobody could taste any of the new harvests before the Nalundiho did so. Wizardry was decried and if caught, a wizard could be killed.

## Economy

Their economy was simple. It was based on subsistence agriculture. They grew millet, sorghum, cassava and a variety of beans. Besides, they reared cattle, goats, sheep and chickens. Generally, there was little trade between them and their neighbours. The trade that occured was organised on a barter system. Land was communally owned on a clan basis and there was enough land for all.

*Bagwe musicians*

# The Banyole

The Banyole live in the Banyole county of Tororo district. They seem to be a sub-group of the Basoga but they are very closely related to the Basamia-Bagwe in customs, language and origin. Like the Bagwe, they claim to have originated from the Banyala of Kenya. Their birth, burial and marriage ceremonies are similar to those of the Basamia-Bagwe with slight variations.

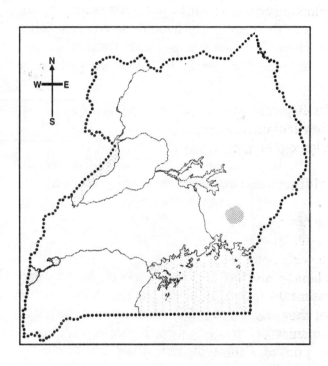

## Birth

When a child was born, the placenta was carried and buried where no one could reach it and use it for evil purposes. It was feared that if the placenta fell into the hands of an evil person, he could manipulate it so as to inflict death or harm on the newly born child or to prevent the mother from ever conceiving again. The mother would remain confined in the house until such a time as the remains of the umbilical cord had broken from the navel. The remains of the umbilical cord were kept in a special gourd and the mother took care to keep as many cords as the children she had. In the event of evil, these cords were believed to be of great importance as an antidote. The food cooked for the mother after giving birth could not be served to any other person save the mother and her husband.

Immediately twins were born, they were just left where they were. Special porridge was administered to the mother and the father and there followed other functions similar to those of the Basamia-Bagwe. The mother could leave the house in special circumstances during the time of confinement. In such an event she would be covered with a winnowing tray before she got out.

## Death

Their death rituals were similar to those of the Basamia-Bagwe in almost all respects. Whenever a man died, three days of mourning (during which there would be no bathing) were observed. In the case of a woman, the days of mourning were four. After either three or four days of mourning as the case may be, the *kasanja* ritual was performed on a road junction to end the mourning and the people would bathe and resume their ordinary business. If one of the twins died, custom forbade mourning and wailing. The Banyole face their dead in the eastern direction which is said to symbolise their possible direction of origin.

## Marriage

When a girl grew up, her parents would ask her for her choice. The girls would then introduce the man to her parents and bride-wealth negotiations would be entered into. Thereafter, due arrangements were made and following a feast, the girl was officially released to go and get married. If one's husband died, the clan would choose of one the late husband's brothers to take her over. If the woman was already elderly, she would remain with her children. The economy and the political systems of the Banyole were similar to those of the Basamia- Bagwe.

# The Bagwere

The Bagwere can be traced to Pallisa district. Their language, *Lugwere* is similar to Lusoga-Lulamogi in many respects.

## Origins

The history of the Bagwere is very sketchy and scanty. Some of their traditions assert that they originated in Bunyoro and first moved to Bulamogi and Bugabula before continuing in present Pallisa district. Their traditions say that they moved from Bunyoro following the disintegration that accompanied the arrival of the Luo and the collapse of the Bachwezi dynasty. Their language and their supposed connection with Bunyoro presupposes that the Bagwere are a Bantu group. Their area of origin may thus be the Katanga region of Central Africa like other Bantu.

## Birth

Whenever a woman was pregnant, she was not supposed to look at the nest of a bird called *Nansungi*. It was believed that if the woman looked at that nest she would miscarry. After giving birth, the woman was not supposed to leave the home. She was given banana leaves to sleep on. Custom demanded that she could not eat from her husband's clan until her days of confinement were over. During this time, she could eat

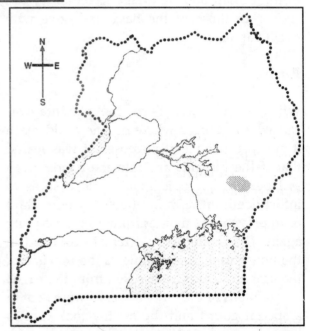

from neighbours or in her parents' home. She was required to eat bananas that were cooked unpeeled and if the piece of banana broke in the process of peeling or eating it, she was not supposed to eat it. Besides the woman was not supposed to look at the sky before the umbilical cord broke off. Otherwise it was feared that the child would die.

## Naming

The naming of the child would wait until the umbilical cord had broken. After the cord had broken, special food was got from the woman's family, usually a banana with *nyondi* still on it. The person going to get this food was not supposed to greet anybody on the way to and from the woman's home. A ritual followed. The child was removed from the house. If the woman had sex with any other man save her husband during the period of pregnancy, the child was not brought out of the house by the doorway. It could be passed through the window or any other opening in the house. The name was given by the grandmother or the aunt of the child. Some names had meanings but some did not.

Whenever a woman gave birth to her first-born child, some food was cooked outside the mother's hut. It was to be eaten by the father and mother of the child. They would in addition, eat some seeds brought from the woman's home. The normal procedure was that if the woman had committed adultery during the time of pregnancy, she could not partake of the food. If the man had committed adultery when the woman was pregnant, he was not supposed to eat this ritual food. His brother or a friend would represent him. Tradition does not have an answer to a situation whereby both the father and mother had committed adultery ·during the period of pregnancy.

## Death

If one died, people would weep and wail loudly. If someone did not cry or cried lightly, he could easily be suspected of having had a hand in the death. If the deceased man was an old man, the people could move singing and mourning and tour the immediate neighbours and on to the well, to take away the spirit of the dead. Normally, the body could not spend two days in the house before being buried. Corpses used to be buried with a needle or mweroko, a small stone used for grinding, to fortify the corpse against body hunters. It was believed that if the body hunters called upon the corpse to come out of the grave, it would reply that it was busy either sewing or grinding, whatever the case may be.

The normal days of mourning were three. They would be ended by a ritual ceremony called okunaba. Herbs would be pounded and mixed in the water. This mixture was then sprinkled on everybody present and on the doorway of the deceased's house. To crown it all, a goat would be slaughtered and eaten. The night before okunaba, the bayiwa (nieces or nephews) would be given a chicken to slaughter and eat because of their significant role during the funeral rites. They were responsible for removing everything that should be removed in connection with the burial and funeral rites. They would also remove whatever rubbish was scattered around and they were customarily paid for it.

The burial of a suicide case differed significantly from that of a normal death. There was no weeping and no prayers offered. A sheep was slaughtered to be eaten by the bayiwa alone perhaps because of the unlucky task of cutting the rope which the bayiwa had to perform. The tree on which the suicide hanged himself had to be uprooted and burnt. If the deceased hanged himself in a house, it was burnt or destroyed however big or good, because such a house was believed to be contaminated by a lot of evil.

## Marriage

In the very early times, parents arranged marriages for their children. However, later, it became customary for a boy to look for a girl. Upon consent, the girl would introduce the boy to her parents. On being introduced, the boy would pay something to the girl's parents not as part of bridewealth, but as a gift. This practice was known as okutona. The process that followed involved the boy inviting the girl's parents to come to his family to assess the bridewealth. They would normally go and assess his wealthy but they could not leave with the cows. This occasion involved a lot of feasting and dancing. The boy's parents would arrange to deliver the bridewealth to the girl's family. The occasion of delivering the bride-wealth was another joyous one accompanied, as it was, with feasting, dancing and merry-making.

After this was completed, the boy's mother, often with another person, would go to fetch the girl from her parents. She would go singing all the way and reach the girl's family round about 8.00 p.m. She would accordingly be given the girl and would return home singing all the way. On reaching the groom's home, the girl was not allowed to sleep with her husband before being washed in the ritual ceremony of *okunabya omugole*. The girl and the boy being married would stand under a tree and bathe in the same water furnished with appropriate herbs. Then, singing, they would prepare to come to the courtyard. On reaching the courtyard, the girl was made to stand before the mother-in-law's door. The mother-in-law would bring a basin of water and pour some on the girl's back. The girl would spread her finger nails out as custom demanded and the old men would inspect her for any signs of pregnancy. Thereafter, the girl's brother would officially hand over the girl to her husband and the girl and her husband would move to their house. The woman could not eat food from her husband's family until she had first eaten food sent from her parents.

## Economy

The Bagwere were an agricultural people and their main crops were millet, *matooke*, potatoes, sorghum, cassava; now, they also grow rice. They grew a large assortment of beans, peas, groundnuts and pumpkins. They also rear cows, goats, sheep and chickens. Their women were not supposed to eat *mamba*

*Bagwere musicians*

(lung-fish), chicken, eggs, and a certain kite-like bird called *wansaka*. In the event of death, any brother of the deceased would inherit his (the deceased's) wife and property. Naturally, it was up to the woman to choose which in-law would inherit her. The real heir to the dead man was usually his first son or any of his sons that proved to be responsible. The Bagwere danced during funerals, especially when the deceased was very old or very important; during wedding ceremonies, particularly before the ritual ceremony of *okunaba*; during instances of merrymaking such as visits and beer parties; and during a ritual dance called *eyonga*. If a woman gave birth to twins she would go with some people to her home to dance eyonga as one of the rituals of inviting the twins into society. The common musical instruments were the *dingidi*, the *tongoli*, drums and *kongo* (thumb piano). The Balingira clan had special drums for particular functions.

# The Bagisu

The Bagisu inhabit the western and southern halves of Mt. Elgon. On the west, the mountain spreads like the fingers of a hand with steep and narrow valleys between them. On the south, the land is broken and consists of a jumble of hills jammed against a high escarpment like a crumpled tablecloth. The escarpment fades gradually to a plain leading away to the northeast inhabited by the Iteso.

## Origins

The Bagisu· have no tradition of an early migration from somewhere. They assert that their ancestors were called Mundu and Sera whom tradition says came out of a hole in Mountain Masaba (Elgon). Their early life seems to have been anti-social, almost based on the principle "survival of the fittest". Very little is so far known about their history but they are known to be related to a sub-group of the Luhya of Kenya known as the Bukusu. The Bagisu are believed to have separated from the Bukusu sometime in the 19th century. The tradition claiming that they have always lived where they are throughout history is not fashionable. The earliest immigrants into Bugisu area are believed to have moved into the Mt. Elgon area during the 16th century from the eastern plains.

Their earliest home is said to have been in the Uasin Gishu plateau of Kenya. They seem to have been an end product of the mixing of peoples of different origins and cultures, but since their language is Bantu, their predecessors should have been Bantu speakers as well.

## Political set-up

The Bagisu had a loose political structure based on clans. Every clan had an elder

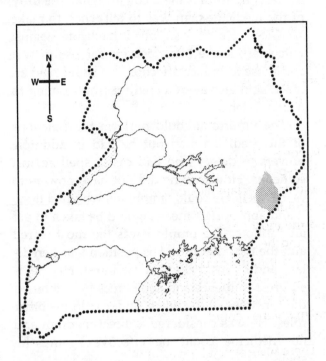

known as *Umwami we sikuka* (chief of the clan). These men were chosen on the basis of age and wealth. They were responsible for maintaining law and order, and unity and the continuity of the clan. They were also responsible for keeping and maintaining the cultural values of the clan and for making sacrifices to the ancestral spirits. Often, stronger chiefs would extend their influence to other clans but no chief managed to subdue. Other clans into one single political entity other important figures in Bugisu included the rainmakers and the sorcerers.

## Witchcraft

The Bagisu have a very strong belief in magic. Their outlook on the most ordinary events was bound up with magic. The experts at magic in Bugisu were divided into three categories. These categories, in their descending order of harmfulness were: the witchdoctor proper or the sorcerer known as *umulosi;* next on the scale is the witch-finder called *umufumu;* and the least harmful is the medicine man. The duty of the medicine man was to tell when to make sacrifices. He also supplied medicine against witchcraft, snake bites, charms for use in war and those to induce affection. He could read an oracle and also avert a creditor from coming to demand debts.

The umufumu could perform the functions of the medicine man but he had in addition, powers to detect who had cast a spell against someone. However, he did not have powers to cast a spell. He could simply tell who had done it and appropriate means would be taken to get an antidote. The umulosi was the most feared and the most harmful. His position was hereditary and he lived alone in the forest. He wielded great influence and sometimes he combined the functions of the witch-finder with his other roles. He was considered a direct medium and no medicine could be effective against his spells.

There were several forms of witchcraft, some particular with men and others particular with women. One of them was called *buyaza.* It was done by putting the backbone of a snake into some belongings of the victim and then calling upon the spirits to attack her/him. Other forms involved various actions and objects but the end result was usually the same, that is inflicting harm or misfortune on the victim. There was another form of witchcraft known as *gamalogo,* which was particular with women and *gamasala* which was particular with men and it required the use of pieces of food leftovers, put in a cocoon of a poisonous cartapillar and placed in the thatch of the victim's hut. The men applied a method called *nabulunga* to bewitch cattle. Another method called *mutabula* was also used by men and it involved burying a small flat woven basket in the ground outside the intended victim's hut. These were just a few. There were several other forms and instances of witchcraft.

## Judicial system

The judicial system was mixed up in their belief in witchcraft. The accused might often be innocent but once named by the witch-finder, he or she had to commit suicide. If a woman was suspected of an evil practice like sorcery, the husband had to send her away and custom demanded that her own people should not accept her either. The person named by the witch-finder was usually killed should he fail to remove the spell which he cast on the victim or if the victim had already died.

The procedure of finding out whether someone had cast the spell took a somewhat strange trend. The accused was summoned and confronted with the corpse or the sick man and urged to confess. If he refused, there were several other ordeals he was subjected to. The commonest was the use of a hot knife. If he got burnt when a hot knife was placed on his body he would be considered guilty of the crime but if he was not burnt, he would be considered innocent. The funny thing about it all was that it was most likely that someone would get burnt when a hot knife was placed on his bare body whether he was guilty or innocent. It is said, however, that there were cases when some people would not get burnt and there used to be living examples to testify to this fact.

## Circumcision

One of the unique social customs of the Bagisu is male circumcision. The actual origin of this practice is mysterious even among the Bagisu themselves. One tradition states that it originated from the demand by the *Barwa* (Kalenjin) when *Masaba,* the Bagisu hero ancestor, wanted to marry a Kalenjin girl. Another tradition claims that the first person to be circumcised had a complication with his sexual organ and that circumcision started as a surgical operation to save the man's life. There is yet another story that the first person to be circumcised had it done as a punishment for seducing other people's wives. Legend states that it was decided to partially castrate him by way of circumcision. When he recovered he resumed his former practices and rumour went around that he had become excellent at it. In order to compete favourably, other men decided to circumcise also.

The Bagisu are a highly superstitious people. Before circumcision, an initiate is administered with a certain herb called *ityanyi*. Its purpose is to arouse interest in circumcision within the candidate. Often the ityanyi is tied round the initiate's big toe or it is put in such a place where he might jump over it unawares. It is believed that if the candidate who has taken the ityanyi is delayed or hindered from being circumcised, he might end up circumcising himself as his mind is said to be so much stimulated towards circumcision that no other thing can distract him.

Circumcision among the Bagisu occurs bi-annually during leap years. Every male has to perform the ritual upon reaching puberty. Those who abscond are hunted down and forcefully and scornfully circumcised. Before the day of circumcision, the initiates are tuned up by having them walk and dance around villages for three days. Their heads are sprinkled with cassava flour and painted with *malwa*-yeast paste. Their relatives dance with them and there is much drumming and singing. Girls, especially the sisters of the initiates, enthusiastically take part in the processions. It is believed that once a boy is circumcised he becomes a true Mugisu and a mature person. An uncircumcised person is known as a *musinde* while a circumcised one is called a *musani*

On the day of circumcision, the initiates are assembled together in a semi-circle. The operation on each initiate is pretty fast. The circumciser and his assistant move around performing the ritual as appropriate. The assistant circumciser pulls the foreskin of the penis and the circumciser cuts it off. The circumciser goes further and cuts from the penis another layer which is believed to develop into another top cover for the penis if it is not removed. The circumciser proceeds and cuts off a certain muscle on the lower part of the penis. These three cuttings end the circumcision ritual.

After circumcision, the initiate is made to sit down on a stool and he is then wrapped in a piece of cloth. After that he is taken to his father's house and made to move around the house before entering it. For three days, the initiate is not allowed to eat with his hands. He is fed. They say that it is because he is not yet fully initiated into manhood.

After three days, the circumciser is invited to perform the ritual of washing the initiate's hands. It is after this ritual that the initiate can eat with his hands. On the same day, the initiate is declared a man. It is then that custom allows him to marry. During the ceremony the initiate is instructed on the duties and demands of manhood. He is informed in addition that agriculture is very important and advised to always behave like a man.

It is believed that the healing of the cuts depends on how many goats have been slaughtered during the initiate's circumcision. After healing, a ritual is performed. All the new initiates in the locality have to attend. This ritual is called *Iremba*. It is an important occasion which all the village people and, these days, even government officials attend. During ritual proceedings, the initiate could pick any girl and have sexual intercourse with her. The girl was not supposed to refuse. It is believed that if a girl refused, she would never

*Bagisu initiates at a circumcision ceremony*

have children when she got married.

Previously, circumcision was done in specific enclosures and only the initiates and the circumcisers were allowed in. The rest of the congregation would just wait and listen from outside the enclosure. Today, however, all people are allowed to watch the whole process. Firmness and courageous endurance on the part of the initiate is appreciated as a sign of bravery.

## Marriage

Traditionally, marriage was arranged by the parents of the boy and the girl, often without the knowledge and consent of the girl. After the bridewealth had been settled, a delegation from the boy's side would come with the boy and they would be offered the bride. A man could marry as many wives as he wished provided he could afford the bridewealth. In the event of divorce, the girl's parents would refund all that they had demanded as bridewealth. This depended on whether the woman left immediately after marriage or if she failed to produce children. If she had had children, only part of the bridewealth was refunded.

## Birth and naming

Birth usually took place in the house. Traditionally, a medicine man would be consulted to administer some medicine in order to lessen the labour pains. Sometimes, the husband would be required to assist the wife during the process of labour. After giving birth, the mother would cut the umbilical cord. The afterbirth was buried.

The naming of the child was not immediate. It would normally wait until such a time as the child began to cry continuously, say throughout the day or throughout the night. Tradition says that an ancestor would then appear as if in a dream and dictate the name by which the child would be called. The name so commanded was normally that of the ancestor who appeared in the dream. The name thus suggested was obligatory and no one was supposed to question its suitability.

## Death

In the event of death, people would cry loudly and the body of the deceased would remain in the house for three days before the burial could take place. This applied to both sexes. Burial took place on the fourth day.

There were elaborate rituals which were performed during burial. If the deceased was barren, a hole was cut at the rear of the house. The corpse would be passed through it to be taken for burial. In the case of a parent, the corpse would be passed through the normal entrance. Women who died unmarried were treated in the same manner as if they had been barren, but such cases were rare because mature girls were normally chased away from their homes by their brothers to go and get married. Before burial, the corpse was entreated that no one present was responsible for its death and therefore its spirit should not return to inflict harm on the living. Barren corpses were also entreated never to return as they had left no trace on earth, and their names were never given to anyone yet to be born.

Enough food and brew was prepared. After the burial a ceremony would be carried out. It was attended by the elders. If the dead person had been the head of the household, this ceremony would involve installing an heir. The rules for choosing an heir demanded that he or she should be well-behaved and understanding. The heir could be a girl or a boy no matter whether he or she was younger than some of his or her elder bothers and sisters.

## Economy

The Bagisu are essentialy an agricultural society. Food production was for subsistence and the main crops included *matooke* (*kamatore*), potatoes (*kamapondi*), millet, beans (*kamakanda*) and peas. Besides agriculture, they also rear some cattle, sheep and goats. Recently, the donkey has become a common sight as a beast of burden. Land was owned on a clan basis. Boys would be allocated pieces of land upon getting married.

# - 4 -

# The Nilotics

The Nilotic group is another extensive family all over East Africa. They can be divided into the Highland-Nilotes and the Plain-Nilotes which in Uganda includes: the Nilo-Hamites (the Karimojong, the Iteso, the Kumam and the Langi); the River-Lake Nilotes (the Acholi, the Alur and the Jopadhola). In Uganda, the River-Lake Nilotes can be described as the Luo.

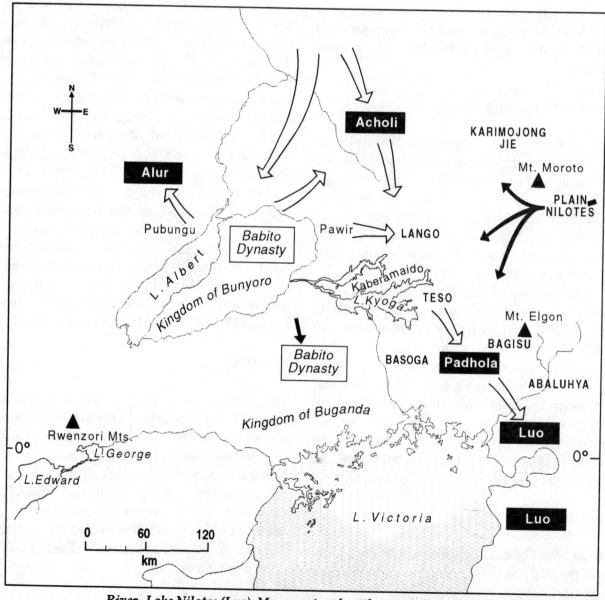

*River- Lake Nilotes (Luo): Movement and settlement in East Africa*

# - 4a -
# The Luo

The Luo are part of the River-Lake Nilotes and are related to the Nuer and the Dinka in the Sudan. Their original homeland is said to have been at Rumbek in southern Sudan. During the 15th century, they were faced with many calamities which forced them to move away in search of new areas for settlement.

Some reasons given for Luo migration include: overpopulation, human and animal diseases, natural hazards like droughts and floods, external pressure from the Galla tribesmen, as well as internal conflicts. Some moved northwards to Shilluk, others moved eastwards to Anuak and some of them continued through Ethiopia, past Agoro Hills to northern Uganda. The major group, however, is said to have moved from Rumbek southwards along the Nile, and settled at Pubungu near Pakwach. This group is said to have been under the leadership of Olum.

Olum had three sons namely: Gapiir (Nyapir), Labongo (Kyebambi) and Tiful. It is said that at Pubungu, Gapiir and Labongo conflicted over the royal spear which was their symbol of power. Thereafter they separated. Gapiir leading a group of people, crossed the Nile and went to the land of the Lendu and Okebu in present West Nile. His people intermarried with the Lendu and Okebu and produced the Alur. The Alur speak Lwo and maintain other elements of Luo culture. Tiful is said to have moved to West Nile also but little is known about his movements and settlements there.

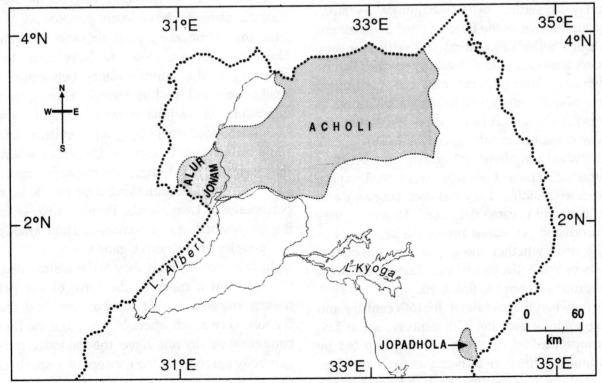

Labongo moved north-eastwards from Pubungu towards present Acholi. In the process, Labongo's group intermarried with and assimilated some Sudanic-speaking peoples in northern Uganda and produced the Acholi. By the beginning of the 18th Century, they were firmly settled in Acholi. There, they encountered the Langi who had been living in Acholi for about two hundred years. Soon conflicts developed between the Acholi and the Langi and this forced the Langi to move southwards to the Lake Kioga region. The Acholi continued to interact and intermarry with the Langi. In the process, the Langi lost their Ateker language and began to speak Luo. They also lost their pastoral element and became settled agriculturalists because the area around L. Kioga was not conducive to pastoralism. Therefore although the Langi speak Lwo, in actual fact, they are not Luo but Nilo-Hamites.

Another group of Luo moved southwards from Pubungu and settled in Pawir which today is settled by the Bagungu. A small group known as the Biito-Luo led by Isingoma Mpuga Rukidi moved on and settled in Bunyoro peacefully and established the Babiito dynasty. Their political influence was limited to a new kingdom which came to be known as Bunyoro-Kitara. It lasted until 1967 when the new constitution introduced by Milton Obote abolished kingdoms in Uganda and set up a republic. Those Luo who went to Bunyoro were assimilated. They lost their language and culture and became Bantuised. However, they introduced pet names among the Banyoro. It is not clear whether there was any interaction between the Bachwezi and Babiito although traditions attempt to link them.

Between the middle of the16th century and the beginning of the 17th century, some Luo groups pushed eastwards. One group led by Adhola, settled in Budama around the first half of the 17th century. They chose to settle in a thickly forested area as a defence against the attacks from their Bantu neighbours who were already settled there. This self-imposed isolation helped them to maintain their language and culture amidst Bantu and Ateker communities. Between 1550 and 1800, other Luo groups crossed into the Nyanza province of Kenya. By 1800, the Luo had completed their migrations and settlement in present north-western, northern and eastern Uganda.

# Effects of the Luo Migrations in Uganda

The Luo migration into Uganda brought about a lot of changes. In the first instance, the Luo migrations marked the last major influx and settlement of Uganda. The migration led to the peopling and settlement of large parts of northern Uganda, West Nile and eastern Uganda.

It was due to the Luo migrations that Uganda came to have such peoples as the Alur, the Acholi, the Jopadhola, and Kumam. These peoples are said to have been the offspring of the intermarriages between the local people and the Luo arrivals. During their migrations in various parts of Uganda, the Luo introduced their language, culture and some animals and crops to the areas where they settled. The Langi, for example, speak Lwo and the Kumam language has a high percentage of Lwo words. Besides, Lwo is an important medium of communication among the peoples of northern Uganda.

In Bunyoro, though they were assimilated, the Lwo left a mark in the form of the pet names, *empaako*, which the Banyoro and the Batooro very much cherish. Although the Luo communities do not have the *empaako*, it is generally agreed that the concept of *empaako* is of Luo origin.

Some historians assert that the Luo introduced the idea of centralised states in Uganda. It is said that the Biito-Luo founded the Kingdom of Bunyoro-Kitara and that Buganda was founded by Kato Kimera who was a twin brother of Isingoma Mpuga Rukidi, the Luo founder of the Babiito dynasty. This assertion is generally correct but it should not be carried beyond its limits to assert that the Luo introduced the idea of centralised states in Uganda. Indeed the Luo movement coincided with the period of state formation in Uganda but the actual idea may not necessarily have come with the Luo. After all, the Batembuzi and the Bachwezi dynasties had existed before the arrival of the Luo.

What is clear is that the Luo founded the Babiito dynasty in Bunyoro-Kitara to replace the collapsing Bachwezi dynasty. One could say with ease, that the Luo had the effect of speeding up the collapse of the Bachwezi. But to assert that they came with the idea of state formation is grossly exaggerated because such an idea was not introduced in those areas where they settled predominantly such as Acholi, apart from chiefdoms.

The Luo are also said to have founded the Baisengobi principalities of Busoga such as Bugabula, Buswikira, Bukasanga and Bukoli. Indeed the connection of these principalities with the kingdom of Bunyoro-Kitara lends emphasis to this assertion. The Luo are also credited with having founded the Rwotdoms (chiefdoms) in Achioli, Lango and West Nile. These seem remarkable achievements but the Luo could as well have borrowed the idea of state formation from the Bantu of the interlacustrine region. In Bunyoro, they were Bantused, while in Acholi, Alur and Jopadhola, they retained their Luo culture and customs.

*Palwo fisherman on the Nile*

# The Acholi

The Acholi are a collection of small ethnic groups brought together by the Luo migration. Historians assert that they are a product of intermarriages between the Luo and the Madi. They are Lwo in language and custom and are closely related to the Alur of West Nile, the Jopadhola of eastern Uganda and the Joluo of Kenya. They inhabit the districts of Gulu and Kitgum which formerly constituted the Acholi district. There are also some Acholi in the southern Sudan.

## Origins

Like other Luo groups, they trace their origin to Rumbek in southern Sudan. It is believed that the major group of the Luo moved downwards under the leadership of Olum and settled at Pubungu near Pakwach.

Legend asserts that Luo was the first man. He had no human parents. He is said to have sprung from the ground. It was taken that his father was *Jok* (God) and that his mother was Earth. Legend adds that Luo's son *Jipiti,* whose mother is unknown, had a daughter called *Kilak*. Kilak was not known to have a husband. Then one time, she got lost in the bush from where she later emerged with a male child. It

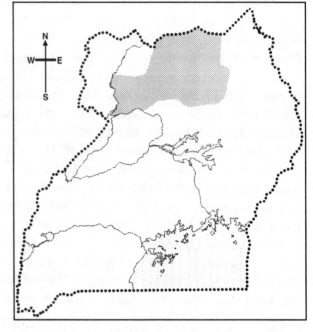

was believed  the father of this child was the devil, *Lubanga*. The child was named Labongo. He was born with bells around his wrists and ankles and he had feathers in his hair. There were definitely magical elements in Labongo. It is said that he was fond of dancing all the time and as he danced the bells jingled.

When Labongo grew up, he married and had a child in the normal way in spite of his peculiarities. Luo's home is said to have been

*Acholi dancers*

at Bukoba, near Pakwach. He possessed an axe which he is said to have driven into the ground and out came the chiefs of many Luo groups. Labongo became the first in the line of the *Rwots* (chiefs) of Payera. The same Labongo whose full title was Isingoma Labongo Rukidi, is also remembered as being first in the line of the Babiito kings of Bunyoro-Kitara. He is said to have been the twin brother of Kato Kimera who is remembered in some quarters as the first in the line of the kings of Buganda. The first Namuyongo of north Bugerere is also said to have been a son of Labongo.

Whether true or false, this legend brings forward the complicated interrelationship between the various peoples of Uganda. It is quite interesting that the Banyoro and the Acholi, different as they seem, could claim common origin. Some groups in Acholi such as the Pajule trace their origin directly to the Bagungu of Bunyoro. It is said that after settling in Pawir, while some Luo (Biito) moved southwards, others also moved northwards and settled in Pajule.

## Birth

The Acholi recognised two distinct birth customs namely the normal birth and the *Jok Anywal* (godly) birth.

## Normal birth

During pregnancy, women were advised not to be away from home. There were no special arrangements for birth and there was no fixed place of delivery. When signs of labour were detected, a *lacol* (midwife) was sent for. The lacol was in most cases an old experienced woman. If a lacol was not available, two of the women present were called upon to assist.

If the expectant woman happened to be inside a hut, she could hold the centre post for support. A woman would support her from behind. The lacol knelt in front of the woman

and, if it was a straightforward birth, she would receive the baby in her outstretched arms. The baby was then washed with cold water. The lacol would then cut the umbilical cord using any available instrument. Knives, spears, arrowheads, bamboo, slices of reed cane or sharpened stones could be used. The remaining part of the cord was tied with a fibre.

The placenta would be buried outside the home, under the woman's granary, in the bush or by the river. Care was taken that the placenta was buried out of reach of those who might use it to charm the child. Among many Acholi clans, the lacol would not touch the ground with her hands when they still contained the blood of the placenta because it was feared in such an event, the mother would become barren. After washing her hands, the lacol would put the mother and the child in the house. If the mother was giving birth for the first time, the house would have been specially constructed for her. Payment for the services of the lacol varied considerably. Sometimes she could render free services but usually, she received a sheep. After the whole process, the lacol was given *awara me lakwany wino* (food or beer) the food would be partly cooked to symbolise the child's birth.

If the woman had problems during the labour, the *won yat* (medicine man) was invited. He would administer the medicine and then rub the back and belly of the woman. A baby who would be forced out in this way was named *Oyat* (boy) or *Layat* (girl). If the won yat failed, the *jwara* (diviner) would be consulted. She would give treatment involving the insertion of a bamboo stick into the woman. She would then hold a chicken by the legs and flutter it around the expectant mother's head while uttering a prayer. As a result of such a struggle, the jwara would direct the umbilical cord to be buried in a special place to appease *Jok*. Then, the child would be given a special name on account of the place where the cord was buried. For instance, *Odwong* (boy) or *Ladwong* (girl) meant that the cord was buried under the odwong tree. *Odur* (boy) or *Ladur* (girl) meant that the cord was buried in the rubbish heap.

The mother and the child would remain in the house for three days if the child was a boy and for four days if the child was a girl. During this period, the mother's food was cooked and brought to her by a young female relative. The food would be saltless because it was believed that if the mother touched salt, the child would go blind. No one was allowed to enter the mother's house during this period, except the cook. If the child's genitals were touched, it was believed, he would grow up to be infertile. Therefore, the mother could only speak to her husband. Besides, she was not supposed to look at the sky otherwise the child would also be impotent. Alcoholic drinks were not allowed into the house. Reasons for this practice varied. Some believed that the child would grow up to be a drunkard; others believed that the child would die. The birth ceremonies varied from clan to clan and even sometimes, from village to village.

## Naming

The child was named after the third fourth day. The process of naming a child went as follows: inside the house would be the mother, the child and some relatives. Then a delegation of the child's maternal and paternal relatives led by the old woman who acted as the midwife would come to the house carrying *odero* (a winnowing tray) in one hand, holding *ogwec* (a knobbed stick used for stirring sim-sim into cooked food) in another hand. In addition, she would also be holding *olobo kwon* (a ladle used for stirring millet bread).

The old woman would knock on the door and in the process of opening it for the delega-

tion, she would suggest a name for the child. There was no criterion for deciding which name the old woman would choose. However, in abnormal circumstances, the mother's choice was given preference. Such a name usually told something about the circumstances of the birth or about the state of the family at the time of birth. For instance, the name *Otto* suggests that many brothers and sisters had died. *Oketch* means that one was born during a famine; *Odoki* suggests that the mother had threatened to go back to her parents; *Bongomin* meant without brothers; *Olanya* means that the mother felt abandoned; and so on.

After all the birth ceremonies, the mother would cease to put on her unmarried girl's belt if that was her first-born. She would begin to be addressed by the name of her first child, e.g. *min Odoki* (mother of *Odoki*). It is then that the woman would become fully accepted into the husband's clan. In some clans, the husband could not eat the food prepared by the new mother for several months. It was also common among Acholi women to refrain from having sex until after weaning the child. All the ceremonies relating to normal births were not addressed to Jok.

## Godly births

The abnormal births were said to be godly. The most common of such births were twins. Others were those born · with physical deformities. They were given special names, for instance, *Ijara* (boy) or *Ajara* (girl) was given to a child with more than five fingers. If the mother was convinced that the deformity was so severe that the child would not grow up to live a useful life, she would drop it in a river as if by accident. Many severely deformed children were killed in this way. When such children lived, they were never abused for fear of Jok's wrath.

When twins were born, various ceremonies were conducted. Such ceremonies are now becoming outdated. The first of them was known as *bilo jok*. The ceremony was conducted around the *abila* (family shrine). Umbilical cords of the twins were cut and put in a baked clay bowl called *laum*. In the morning when the ceremony would be performed, the laum together with the other objects which were used during the twins' birth were placed by the abila. The mother sat on a skin with her back to the abila and her legs outstretched. The first-born of the twins was placed on her mother's lap nearest to her while the second born was put on her knees.

The people present would stand in line in the order of their age and offer prayers and sacrifices in the abila. After this, the leader of the ceremony would hold a white cock and allow it to flap' its wings violently over the mother and twins. This act was repeated in turn by everyone present. The feathers that flew out from the cock would be stuck into the ground beneath the abila or beneath the *okongo* tree. Then a white hen was also brought and a similar process was repeated. Then, one by one, the people would dip their hands into a calabash full of water and sprinkle it over the mother and twins. Besides, they would also smear the necks and bellies of the mother and her twins with *moo yaa* (oil from the *yaa* tree). With this, the ceremony would be over. The mother was then lifted up with the skin on which she had been sitting, with her twins still on her lap and carried into the hut. The women present would then go through the motions of making love to the father of the twins making jokes that they would also like to have twins. Thereafter, people would go out to drink and dance.

## Religion

The Acholi believed in a supreme being called *Jok*. The shrine for Jok was known as the *abila*. All sacrifices, private and public, were offered inside the abila. The spirits of the dead were believed to appear near the abila. However, these spirits had no permanent dwellings. They were believed to wander about and thereafter to appear by signs. They were worshipped so that they could assist the bereaved ones or exercise their power to make hunting successful or scare the evil spirits away from the village. They were believed to help the surviving members of the families if they were treated well. Accordingly, they were offered meat, pudding, simsim and beer during the appropriate times of the sacrifices at the abila.

It is interesting to note that there was the christian idea of God among the Acholi as *Jok*. However, when the missionaries came, they forced the Acholi to adopt the concept of *Lubanga* to represent God. Formerly, among the Acholi, the term Lubanga or *Lubaya* was used to mean death or evil. Lubanga was known to cause evil and to kill people. Every bad thing was attributed to Lubanga just as every good thing was attributed to Jok . No huts or shrines were built for Lubanga in the villages. Sacrifices, or 'cooking' for Lubanga was done outside the village and the dung of fowls was often added in his food as another step to degrade him. Yet this same Lubanga is now the idea of God which the Christians forced the Acholi to adopt.

## Acholi Dances

The Acholi usually sing about everyday incidents but some of their songs refer to well known incidents in the past. Songs are tuneful and dancing is communal. Solo dancing is rare.

*Bwola dancers from Kitgum district, 1992*

The Acholi have eight different types of dances namely: *lalobaloba, otiti, bwola, myel awal (wilyel), apiti, ladongo, myel wanga* and *atira*.

In the *lalobaloba* dance, no drums are used. The people dance in a circle. The men form the outer ring. A man may move and hold a girl's hand above his head. There are no special occasions for this dance. All dancers carry sticks.

In the *otiti* dance, all male dancers carry spears and shields. The dancers encircle drums which are usually attached to a post in the middle of the arena. This dance involves more shouting than singing; in the end, spears and shields are put down and the dance is converted into lalobaloba.

The *bwola* dance is the most important. It is the chief's dance and is only performed on his orders. The men form a large circle and each of them carries a drum. The movement of the feet matches rhythmically with the beating of the drums. The girls dance separately inside the circle without beating the drums. The dance has a definite leader and he moves by himself within the circle. He sets the time and leads the singing. He is considered an

*An Acholi man playing* okeme *(thumb piano)*

*An Acholi dance leader*

important person and traditionally he was among the few people the community allowed to wear a leopard skin.

The *myel awal* dance was a funeral dance. The women wail around the grave while the men, armed with spears and shields dance lalobaloba. *Apiti* was a dance for the girls. Men were not supposed to participate. The girls danced in a line and sang. It was usually held in the middle of the year when the rains were good.

*Ladongo* was danced following a successful hunt when the hunters were still away from their homes. In this dance, men and women faced each other in two lines and jumped up and down clapping their hands. In the *myel wanga* dance, all men sat down and played their *nanga* (harps) while in front of them, the women danced apiti. This dance was usually held after marriages or at beer parties. Then there was the *atira* dance. It is now completely outdated. It was held on the eve of a battle. All the dancers were armed and they went through the motion of spear fighting and thrusting.

## Political set-up

Although the colonialists preferred to rank the Acholi among the stateless societies, the Acholi had a system of centralised government. They were organised in chiefdoms each under a hereditary ruler known as the *Rwot*. The Rwot was a central figure and he had judicial, executive and legislative powers. In addition, he was the link between the living and the dead. It was his duty to offer sacrifices to the ancestors on behalf of his people.

The society possessed chiefly regalia such as drums, spears and stools. The administrative structures were not well stratified. The general political organisation could be likened to that of the pre-colonial kingdoms of Buganda, Bunyoro, Nkore, Toro and Buhaya states of Karagwe. In fact the larger chiefdoms such as Payera and Padibe were bigger and more organised than some of the smaller pre-colonial kingdoms of the south.

## Economy

The Acholi practised mixed farming. They kept cattle, goats and sheep as well as fowls in addition to practising agriculture. The main food crops included sorghum, millet, simsim and a wide assortment of beans. They supplemented this with hunting.

The Acholi practised various types of hunting. The first of such types of hunting was *line*. It took place during the dry season in December. Another type was *dwar arum*. This took place in the dry season when there was no grass and it involved a lot of hunters. The third type was *dwar obwo*. This was an ordinary type of hunt with nets and spears and it also involved a lot of hunters and dogs. Another type of hunting was called *kirange*. It was held during the early rainy season when the rivers would be slightly flooded. The game was driven into the rivers and speared in the water.

Normally, there was little opportunity for hunting during the rainy season because no organised hunting could take place. During this time, only the *okia* (trappers) could go out after the animals. Their work was quite difficult because they worked alone. They used different traps according to the type of animal that was to be trapped. The common traps included *okol* (running a noose attached to a log of wood); *tekke* (a circular foot trap; *bur* (a pit dug in the game's path); and *tong twok* (the falling spear trap used to kill an elephant which passed under the tree from which the spear was suspended). The majority of the other traps were intended for smaller animals and birds.

**Dr. Martin Aliker: one of the cultural heads (Rwot) of Acholi**

# The Alur

The Alur are one of the various ethnic groups that inhabit the West Nile part of Uganda. They live amongst the Okebu, Lendu, Kakwa, Aringa and other ethnic groups of West Nile. However, unlike their neighbours who are Sudanic, the Alur are Luo. They are Nilotics and they belong to the same language group as the Acholi, the Jopadhola, the Joluo of Kenya, the Shilluk, the Anuak and other Luo of the southern Sudan.

## Origins

Alur tradition states that they migrated from the southern Sudan with the other Luo following the Nile banks. Their original homeland is said to have been Rumbek on the confluence of the Nile and the Bahr-el-Ghazel rivers. They moved south along the Nile to Pubungu whence they dispersed, some moving on to Bunyoro, others to Acholi, yet others to eastern Uganda and on to the Nyanza province of Kenya, while the Alur moved westwards to West Nile. Historians claim, however, that the Alur are not purely Luo, but that they are a product of intermarriages between the Luo, the Lendu and the Okebu. But since the Alur maintained the Lwo speech and other Luo customs they should be grouped that way.

## Legend

The Alur legend of origin says that there once lived a great king called *Atira*. He is said to have been a direct descendant of God and that when he died, his son *Otira* succeeded him. *Otira* is said to have in turn been succeeded by *Opobo*. *Opobo* ruled from a place called Nyirak in Lango country. When Opobo died, he left three sons: *Tiful*, *Nyapir* and *Labongo*.

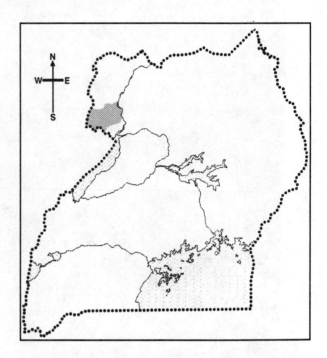

One day, Nyapir borrowed Labongo's spear intending to spear an elephant. Unfortunately, the elephant went away with the spear. When the news reached Labongo, he was annoyed and he insisted on having back his own spear in spite of Nyapir's pledges to offer him a substitute. Therefore, Nyapir decided to follow the elephant and, having crossed a big river, he found himself in a cool beautiful land.

During his wanderings in this land, Nyapir encountered an old woman. The old woman is said to have taken him to a place where, among other spears, Nyapir was able to recognise Labongo's spear. The old woman gave him a bead.

When he reached home, he called all his brothers and presented the spear. Everyone was amazed at Nyapir's story, more especially, at the bead. The bead was handed over for everyone to see and, in the process, an infant son of Labongo accidentally swallowed it.

*Alur drums*

Nyapir had got his revenge. He also demanded that his own bead be given back. He refused all other possible substitutes. Left with no alternative, Labongo handed over the child to Nyapir to open and retrieve the bead. Nyapir killed the child and got out the bead. This act is said to have annoyed all the brothers so much that they decided to separate.

Tiful, having been impressed by Nyapir's story of a good country beyond the river, moved with his followers including the Lendu and Okebu to the highlands in the west. His descendants are said to comprise the Alur of Zaire. Nyapir followed Tiful and travelled along the west bank of the Victoria Nile and finally camped with his followers in an area opposite Pakwach. The land was not good for grazing and there being no salt licks his cattle began to stray away.

One day, some of the cows which had previously disappeared came back on their own and they were discovered to have salt particles adhering to their hooves. Nyapir gathered together his people and followed the track of the cows into the highlands of West Nile. He left behind one of his sons called Dosha to rule Pakwach. Nyapir then established himself in the West Nile highlands.

Historians contend, however, that this story of the Alur's entry into West Nile, as conceived in the legend of the spear and the bead, was actually a struggle for power between the two brothers over the spear, which was part of their chiefly regalia. When they entered West Nile, they are said to have mixed with the Lendu and Okebu as well as with the Sudanic Madi in the north and later on with the Nyai, the Bendi, and the Bira to the southwest.

*A traditional Alur homestead*

## Religion

The religious rituals of worship among the Alur were cultivated and protected by the *Bandwa*, the *Jupa Jogi* and the *Jupa Jok*. These were, in effect, the Alur equivalents of the clergy. The equivalent of God was known as *Jok*. The manifestations of Jok were more often than not in personal terms. Thus, Jok could be male or female, young or old, and so on. But sometimes Jok could be conceived of in non-personal forms, for instance, as a situation. The ultimate nature of Jok, however, was quite unknown.

Among the Alur, worship was not routine such as every morning, evening or on Sundays and Fridays. It was necessitated by misfortunes of one kind or another which required that Jok should be appeased. The Alur believed that misfortunes or diseases were not natural consequences. To them, misfortunes and diseases were caused and the causes took different forms. Spiritual entities or dead ancestors could demand attention, food, beer,

meat and some other forms of comfort by inflicting punishments on the living in terms of deadly diseases, misfortunes or some slight sickness which, if not recognised and appropriately attended to, could become dangerous. This could take the form of dumbness, paralysis of the body or just part of it, mental breakdown, etc.

In the event of a misfortune like sickness, the family head together with a brother or two associates would go to a diviner known as *Julam bira, Jolam wara* or *Ajoga* to have the misfortune diagnised. The diviner would employ the various instruments at his disposal to trace the cause of the trouble. He would then advise on the appropriate measures to take to avert the misfortune. Misfortune was said to be caused by evil spirits or by evil persons who, by use of magic, could harm an otherwise healthy person.

## Ritual marriage

The Alur had a sort of religious marriage which was conveyed in the *mukeli gagi* rituals. The actual ceremony took the following form:-

Sometimes, a married woman could be afflicted by the ancestral spirits of her own people. In such an event, her husband would get cowrie shells and take them to her home. There, the shells would be tied to the pole of her father's ancestral shrine. The husband would, in effect, be pledging to pay two goats, male and female, in order to rescue the cowrie shells because such shells were not supposed to remain at his father-in-law's home for ever.

If the husband was already initiated into the religious cult, he would go to rescue the shells himself. However, if he was not yet initiated, he would not be allowed to go because a lot was involved which he, as a non-initiate, was not supposed to know. But if he was willing to be initiated there and then, he could go. In fact most husbands preferred this alternative because at the end of the ritual, the woman would cease to be his wife if he was not yet a confirmed believer. Sexual relations with the former husband would stop forthwith if he was not yet a confirmed believer.

If the initial husband hesitated to be initiated, the woman would ritually be married to another man who was already confirmed and who consented to have her as a ritual wife. The ritual husband would consider her to be his wife and would even go ahead and have children with her.

## Ritual joining

The actual ritual started late in the evening when the believers would sing to alert the people in the vicinity. The woman would be made to sit in the centre of a circle and, after showing signs of being possessed, she would be led to a place of her own choice where a goat would be slaughtered and eaten. Another goat would be given to the believers to be slaughtered and eaten.

The husband and the wife were then made to lie down on a papyrus mat facing each other. The man was then asked to throw one of his hands and legs on the woman and the woman was asked to assume the posture and both would then be asked to proceed to play sex. This process was known as *ariba* (joining). Thereafter, the couple would be given grass stems to break simultaneously. This woman would have power over that man's other wives if they were not ritually joined to him. If the husband was not the initial one, he would proceed to pay bridewealth for his new wife. If, later on, the initial husband became confirmed, he would retrieve his wife. If the ritual husband had already had children with her, he was not supposed to complain. He was supposed to treat them well in the hope that he might himself also one day be ritually married to another man's wife with whom he might as well have children.

## Economy

The Alur were settled agriculturalists. Their main crops included millet, sorghum, cassava, simsim, potatoes and a variety of beans. Now, they also grow cotton and coffee. Besides, they kept goats, chickens, cattle and sheep.

*Grain stores of the Alur*

# Jopadhola

Jopadhola live in eastern Uganda amidst various Bantu ethnic groups. They are said to have settled there since the middle of the 16th century. They are surrounded on all sides by the Bantu and the Nilo-Hamitic peoples. To the west live the Banyole and the Basoga; to their north and east live the Bagwere and the Iteso; and to their south live the Basamia and the Bagwe.

## Origins

The Jopadhola are Luo. They have similar traditions of origin with the Alur, Acholi and the Joluo of Kenya. It is said that before moving to western Kenya, the Luo first settled in southern Busoga for some time. The earliest Luo migrants settled in the Kaberamaido peninsula where they were joined by more Luo migrants from Pawir in Bunyoro. Then some immigrants from Bugwere, Teso and Busoga came towards the Kaberamaido peninsula in the second half of the 18th century. This forced the Jopadhola to extend to the south and later on to the east. The land they occupied was previously vacant and this helped them to maintain their traditional culture free from foreign influences. Thus, unlike the Biito-Luo who were Bantuized and assimilated in Bunyoro, the Jopadhola were able to maintain themselves as a distinct Luo group amidst the various Bantu and Nilo-Hamitic societies.

## Religion

Like the Acholi, the Lugbara and the Langi, the Jophadhola conceived of *Jok* as a supreme being. However, they did not take it as far as

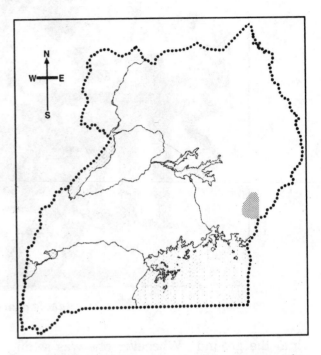

the Acholi and the Langi did. Among the Jopadhola, the concept of Jok was later merged into the Bantu belief in *Were,* a super-being whose chief services to mankind were mainly connected with fertility.

Jopadhola traditions assert that they have always believed in one supreme being called Were. In physical terms, Were was conceived of as a white, merciful, and good being who could manifest himself in various ways. As god of the courtyard known as Were *Madiodipo,* he was believed to take care of the home and the family. As god of the wilderness, known as *Were Othin,* he was believed to guard and guide men when they went hunting, fighting or on a journey.

In every home a shrine was built for Were. On each side of the shrine, two white feathers were planted into the ground. Every morning, the owner of the home would open the gate and approach the shrine to tell Were to make the day "as bright  as these feathers planted

*Adhola dancers performing*

into the ground". Whenever one was setting out on a journey, he would approach his shrine to ask Were to make the journey "as peaceful as this shrine".

Beside Were, the Jophadhola believed in the cult of Bura. The concept of Bura is said to be foreign to the Jopadhola. It was introduced by someone called Akure from Bugwere. Tradition says, however, that it was not Akure but his nephew Majanga who turned the cult into a universal institution among the Jopadhola. Furthermore, it was under Majanga's leadership that the Jopadhola clans were consolidated. This unification enabled the Jopadhola to offer resistance to Kiganda and British imperialism at the beginning of the 20th century.

## Marriage

Traditionally, the parents of the boy would identify a girl for him and make arrangements for marriage. The formula governing such identification took into account the girl's conduct, that of her parents, the physical strength of the girl, her beauty, and the ties of kinship between the girl's and the boy's families. They were supposed to belong to clans which had no ties of kinship whatsoever. Having identified the girl, the boy's parents would consult with the girl's parents. If the latter consented, the girl was earmarked as a way of engagement. The traditional method of doing it was by putting a traditional ring on the girl's finger or a necklace around her neck. This would alert other would-be contenders to the fact that the girl was already engaged.

Where the above-mentioned method was not appropriate, another one would be applied. Here, boys of the same age group would identify a particular girl, waylay and forcefully carry her to the home of the particular boy who desired her for marriage. The boy would proceed to sleep with her and that would be the end. She would in effect become his wife and further arrangements

*A modern Adhola dancer*

would be made to settle matters with the girl's parents.

Whatever the circumstances, payment of bridewealth was a normal consequence. The boy's parents had to pay at least five cows, six goats, a cock, a knife, barkcloth, salt and meat. Upon being handed over to the boy for marriage, the girl would spend seven days of confinement in the hut. During that time, she would be fed on pea stew as the principal meal. After this period of confinement, the clan elders would gather and the bride would be formally introduced to them. The norms of the new family and the clan at large were impressed upon her through lectures. After all the bridewealth had been paid, the girl would receive from the parents a goat, several chickens, millet flour and a wide assortment of other gifts. Marriages among the Jopadhola were essentially polygamous, the limit being set by age and bridewealth obligations.

## Birth

During pregnancy, the woman would not use certain types of wood for cooking or lighting fires. She would not eat particular types of food. The names of snakes or of the dead were not to be mentioned in her presence. Besides, no man except the woman's husband was supposed to pass behind her whenever she was seated. He might cause her a miscarriage or some other misfortune, it was believed.

The woman would give birth in her own hut. Traditional midwives or her mother-in-law would attend to the delivery. Banana leaves fetched from a specific species of bananas would be used for her bedding. The woman would remain confined in the house for four days, if the child was female and for three days if the child was male. During the days of confinement, she would bath herself with only cold water in which some herbs would be mixed for her health and for the

*A typical traditional Adhola homestead*

health of the child. Besides, she was also fed on pea stew with porridge as her first meal in the morning during this period of confinement. If the newborn child was a boy, sacrifices of hens or goats would be offered to the god responsible for the fertility of women.

After the normal days of confinement, the child would be named. The grandfather of the child would name it. The naming ceremony was a big feast punctuated by a lot of eating and drinking and it was in some way, a means of accepting the child into the clan. The children were often named after their ancestors. Therefore, during the naming ceremony, the ancestors were invoked to accept the name of the child and indeed the child itself, into the clan.

If the woman gave birth to twins both the mother and the father of the twins, would not leave the house for seven days. The uncle of the twins would not leave the house for seven days. The uncle of the twins would welcome them into the world by offering the mother food, drinks and other ritual gifts. No one would touch, greet or talk to the parents of twins without giving them a gift.

## Death

Whenever a person died, the corpse would stay overnight in the house. A long drum would be played at night and the corpse was bathed and wrapped in barkcloth. A cow was normally slaughtered near the grave in order to go with the deceased and feed him with milk in the world of the dead. The people would make a fire and keep sleeping outside until *kongo*, a traditional drink, was brewed and a ceremony held to end the days of mourning. No one would have a bath for at least three days after someone's death.

# - 4b -
# The Highland Nilotics

This group of people is mainly concentrated in Kenya with the Kalenjin as the largest group. It extends to central Tanzania to include the Dadog and Otiek. In Uganda, only t he Sebei belong to this group.

## The Sebei

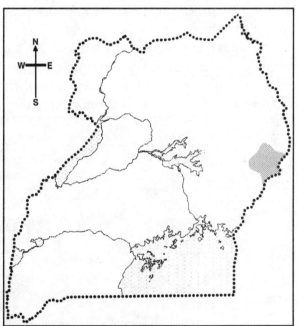

The Sebei inhabit the present Kapchorwa district. The land stretches from the cold heights of Mt. Elgon to the hot plains of Karamoja. Along these plains, the Sebei have been subjected to the influx of the Kitosh from Kenya.

### Origins

The exact origins of the Sebei are still difficult to trace. Their original homeland could have been in the Ethiopian direction. They might have first settled in the neighbourhood of the Suk hills before finally occupying their present area. They were so much removed from the rest of Uganda that during the colonial days, they were governed under the Outlying Districts' Ordinance.

### Social set-up

The Sebei are very proud of their individuality and customs. One of their unique customs that distinguishes them from the rest of their neighbours is female circumcision. The Sebei circumcise both boys and girls. Male circumcision is also practised by their Bagisu neighbours but with marked differences in the arrangements and actual ceremony.

### Female circumcision

While male circumcision was very well organised and carried out after every two years, female circumcision was an annual event requiring not so much organisation except the availability of sufficient *wambi* (maize) to make sufficient beer for the occasion. This was usually in December but no fixed dates were laid down.

The girls to be circumcised were usually between the ages of thirteen and sixteen years, and they had to be virgins. If a girl became pregnant before circumcision, it was usual to circumcise her immediately after her condition became known without the formal ceremonies. Circumcision was a way of initiation into womanhood and no girl could be allowed to enjoy her full rights, including sexual intercourse, before she had been circumcised.

The beginning of the ceremony was announced by small groups of girls who would start dancing from home to home. They were led by a young woman of between twenty and thirty years who would be chosen on the basis of the prestige she had attained when she endured circumcision without complaint during her own turn.

The initiates were decently dressed. In the recent past, they could wear cotton blouses and skirts held up by crossed straps over their shoulders. Before the actual ceremony, they would sing and dance for almost two days. They ere not, but they could be, allowed to drink milk and take short rests if they became particularly distressed.

Late in the afternoon of the day of the ceremony, their faces were decorated in the form of squares with coalin in order to increase their beauty. After sunset, a large crowd of people would gather and form a circle around the initiates. Old women would step into the circle to sing songs in praise of circumcision and to urge the girls to endure all the pain of circumcision without fear or complaint. The initiates would then join hands

*A Sabiny woman in a traditional dress*

*Constructing a house in Sebei*

in pairs and extend to the edges of the circle where they would slightly touch the onlookers with the cows' tails or tree branches to show that they had no fear of anybody or anything. The men would be in the neighbourhood, drinking beer. While drinking beer they used long tubes with filters at the bottom. Merry-making would go on throughout the night.

## The act of circumcision

The girls were circumcised just after dawn. The girls and their female relatives would assemble at the place of operation. Customarily, no man could attend but any woman or girl could. The initiates were made to lie down with their arms above their heads and their legs spread. They were not supposed to be tied or held during the operation.

Just before circumcision, the intestines of a sheep which had been slaughtered for the occasion were laid on the face of the girls to keep their eyes open during the operation. Then the circumciser would perform the act by making three separate incisions into each girl. Thereafter the girls were led into a fenced *boma* across the entrance of which the entrails of the

slaughtered sheep were laid. On each side of the entrance were placed two spears pointing outwards from the *boma*, only leaving sufficient space for one person to enter. The slaughtered sheep and the spears were to scare away evil spirits. Legend has it that in the olden days these stab were used by parents to spear girls who refused to be circumcised.

Once the girls were inside the *boma*, people were allowed to visit them. About an hour after the ceremony, the initiates were led away to huts and put in the care of old women until they would recover in one or two months' time. It was urine that was used for treating the wounds. After recovery, the girls were regarded as ripe and eligible for marriage and able to enjoy other privileges accorded to women.

## Economy

The Sebei were pastoralists by nature and even today, the *Basiboro* (*Konjek*) section of them are still pastoral. On the Greek river plain, the influence of the Kitosh brought about the practice of maize-growing. Now, they also grow coffee which was introduced into their land from Bagisu.

# - 4c -
# The Nilo-Hamites

These people are often referred to as the Plain Nilotes. In Uganda, they constitute the Atekerin or the Lango group which includes the Karimojong, the Iteso, the Langi, the Kumam and the Kakwa. Their origins can be traced to the northeast, probably the Kaffa region of Ethiopia. During their migrations, the whole group is said to have first settled in Karamoja. From there they moved south to occupy Teso, Lango and Kumam. Some of them, like the Langi, lost their original language and some cultural traits due to Luo influence. However, some of their peculiarities in custom and culture can still be identified.

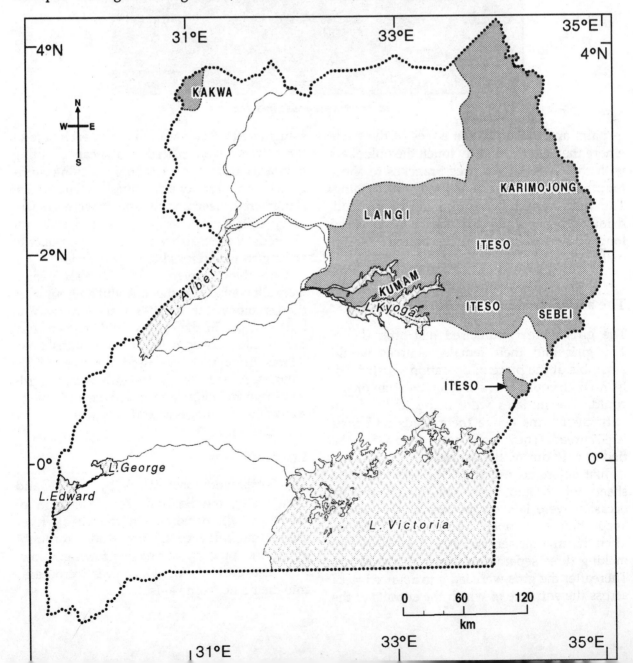

# The Langi

The Langi belong to the Lango family which also comprised the Iteso and the Kumam, the Labwor, the Jie (Lango-Olok) and the Karima-jong (Lango-Dyang).

## Origins

Tradition asserts that the Langi originated from Mt. Otukei, also called Mt. Awil. They claim that they came from mountains which had abundant rain. This land could be Kaffa and this presupposed indeed that the Langi originated from Abyssinia. Their original homeland was north of Lake Turkana where they used to live along with the Jie and the Karimojong. This means, by implication, that the Langi are also related to Dodoth, Lotuko, Toposa, and the Turkana of Kenya. Together with the Iteso, Kumam and Karimojong, they comprise the Atekerin family in Uganda.

## Religion

The Langi believed in a spiritual being called *Jok*. Jok was a super being and a wider concept manifested into *Jok-Lango* who specialised in diseases which had little or nothing to do with demon-possession. All demon-possession fell under the sphere of *Jok-Man*. Other manifestations of Jok included *Jok-Atida* and *Jok-Orongo*. Though spiritual, Jok was taken as an individual entity, not a particular manifestation. He could sometimes be taken to mean the devil with powers to make people contract diseases or meet undesirable fates. In their human form these joggi (plural) were believed to be in several respects like human beings for they were mortal, male or female, and their society was believed to uphold marriage and decry adultery. They were said to  celebrate birth

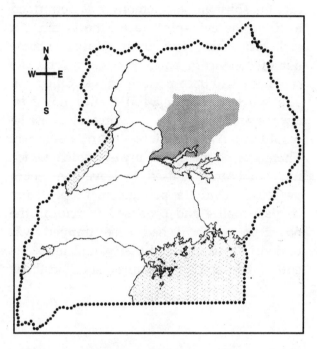

and to weep for their dead.

In their human form, they were said to have long, curly, tangled hair, a black or slightly brown skin, sometimes tarnished by dust. However, they would be different from human beings in that what was fair to them was foul to human beings and vice versa. For instance, their most delicious food was said to be houseflies.

The Langi were not much concerned with the world after death. What was clear to them was that when a person died, his spirit did not die but went to the world of the dead. Nothing was known about this world except that the souls of the people who had died with grief or who had been crudely murdered, or who had died in bitter resentment against their relatives, could ally with the evil Joggi and acquire the power to haunt those against whom they had grudges.

Every Lango family had an ancestral shrine

be offered to propitiate the relevant Joggi. This was important because the evil spirits could possess any one of their relatives. In the event of such a happening a sheep was killed to placate the spirit and a ceremony was performed to drive the evil spirit out of the victim. An evil spirit which stubbornly refused to come out of the victim whenever the appropriate ceremony had been performed was called *cen*. The witch doctor (*ajwaka*) could, however, always get the better of it and in such a case he would trap it and seal it in a pot or a calabash. There was no mercy for any evil spirit which had stubbornly refused to leave the victim peacefully. Once trapped, unless it repented of its past malice and promised to reform, the object in which it had been trapped was buried in a swamp and that would mark the end of that spirit. Sometimes, such obstinate

*Lango traditional war dress*

spirits, it is said, could even be speared to death.

When it was time for sowing, the Langi would invoke the power and blessing of Jok by a ceremony called *rubo koti* (the mixing of seeds). This ceremony was often accompanied by the sacrifice of a chicken or sheep, the throat of which would be cut and the blood allowed to drip onto the seeds. It was believed that in the absence of this ceremony, the seeds would not germinate.

## Dwellings

The Langi dwelt in villages. A village could contain more than a hundred huts built in a line. In front of the huts, there was a line of granaries belonging to the individual families. Beyond them, at a distance, was the communal cattle kraal.

When someone needed a new site on which to build a hut, he would take a chicken and some beer to the desired site and leave them there for a day or two. If on his return he found that something had eaten the chicken or drunk the beer, he would abandon the site as it was considered an ill-omen. For fear of evil spirits, the Langi avoided building near swamps and also avoided building near stony or rocky ground.

The huts were of different types. An *iguruguru* was a small hut intended for sleeping in as a guest house. It was, made with a low doorway that people had to enter crawling. The purpose of the low doorway was to prevent enemies from aiming their spears at the people sleeping during the night. The unmarried youth slept in small huts called *otogo* whose doorways, approached by means of a ladder, were only big enough to allow a person to crawl in and out. This type of hut is now very rare but it had its entrance closed by a grass mat and is said to have been very warm inside.

*A traditional Lango hut*

## Implements

Formerly, the implements of the Langi were few and simple. As a bed, they used a hide which was usually stretched on a raised floor in the hut. The women's utensils included various pots, a pan, calabashes, drinking vessels, brooms, pestles and mortars, plus a number of grinding stones. The man had his spear, a shield, a knife, a hunting net, a drum and a hoe. Among his favourite implements was a drinking stick which looked much like an ordinary stick but was in fact hollow with a sucking tube inside.

## Dress

The Langi were not used to wearing clothes but they were fond of personal adornments. When they still lived in Karamoja, the men went completely naked. The women used to wear *ajoo* (a skin). When the Langi came into contact with the Acholi during the Luo migrations, they adopted the Acholi ways of dressing and also dropped their Ateker language and spoke Lwo. The men of the *Jo-Aber* clan were the first to wear goat-skins

*Young Langi girls in village setting*

pioneers in rejecting their traditional *ajoo* in favour of the *apronon*. It was in recent times that the other Langi men of the south and west started to wear skins; until then, they used to go stark naked.

## Personal adornments

The Langi girls were tattooed both on the back and front. Men were only tattooed on the back. The two lower front teeth were removed and the ears were pierced in as many as ten points to provide accommodation for *gilo* beads. Metallic ornaments were worn in the nose and the upper lip. Often the lower lip was also pierced to accommodate such objects as took the owner's fancy. Piercing was sometimes extended to the tongue to enable it to accommodate a two-beaded ornament.

On their arms and legs, they wore a large quantity of bracelets both above and below the knees and elbow and round their ankles and wrists. Their necks were also encased in another pile of bracelets rendering them almost stiff. Their women usually rubbed roasted simsim on their heads and twisted their hair. Both men and women were fond of smearing their bodies with oil or ghee. Often, the men would work their hair into elaborate headdresses as the Jie and the Karimajong have been doing recently and some still do. They would plaster themselves with mud and stud them with beads. Women were also fond of wearing a big brass ring on the wrist and during quarrels, they frequently hit each other on the head with these big brass rings.

## Political set-up

Lango society was segmentary. Leadership was centred around the clan which would be both a kinship unit and the basic constituency of politics within the Rwotdom. The *Rwot* (chief) had the duty of controlling the entire clan. He was helped by a council of elders. The other senior members besides the *Rwot* were the leading elders of the clan. The council of elders was responsible for general administration and the maintenance of law and order within the clans. They organised the payment of debts, *luk* (adultery and fornication fines) as well as bridewealth . This council was also responsible for organising the distribution or disposition of the property of the deceased.

Many clan elders were usually brought together to form the *Odonge-Atekere* and one of them would be elected *Rwot* or *Awitong* as he was also called. The *Odonge-Atekere* were the clan branch leaders and the *Rwot* had the duty of controlling all the affairs of the clan. He led the warriors to war and mobilised defence

*Traditional Lango headdress*

during an invasion. After battle, he organised a feast during which the *moo* and *moi* (military ranks) were conferred upon those that deserved them. These ranks were for those who had displayed excellent performances during the battle.

## Military

The society had no standing army. All able-bodied men were considered warriors. Before war could be declared, a foreteller would be consulted to predict the results of the war. If luck was proven, old women would spit into the hands of the warriors and they would then set off. The leaves of the *olwedo* tree were put in the path where the warriors passed to enhance their luck in the impending fight.

War booty was normally retained by whoever looted it. After the war, a ceremony was convened in which to award the *moi* ranks. The person who killed a big or important person was styled *Anuko*; his privileges and other titles were increased by making tattoo marks on his left shoulder and neck. The highest moi was *Abwangor*. During this ceremony, a goat was slaughtered while the elders stood in front of the family shrines and its blood was allowed to drip on the warriors. The goat was then skinned and its meat divided accordingly.

## Judicial system

The judicial system of the Langi was harsh by modern standards because in certain instances, offenders could be dealt with on the spot by whoever caught them. For instance, there was no case to answer if a man speared another one to death after having found him sleeping with his wife. There was nothing like manslaughter since a murderer would be killed if he was caught. So also could a notorious thief. As for the latter, he could even be killed by his own people.

Often, on the intervention of elders, murder could be compensated in the form of goats, cows or a young girl. If the murdered person was a man and the girl who would be surrendered as compensation gave birth to a boy, she would be set free and returned to her people. If she had proved good, she would be married to a young man within the clan and bridewealth would accordingly be paid. Murder victims were almost always men since it was considered cowardly to kill a woman or a child.

If a woman killed her husband, she would be returned to her people and the bridewealth would be refunded. She would in addition be required to pay compensation. The women had a lesser role than men to play in society except as sources of wealth and custodians of the rituals of birth and divination.

Other offences in the Lango society included pre-marital pregnancies and fornication.

if the boy refused to marry the girl and the girl died in labour, the case was tantamount to murder. If she successfully delivered, the child would remain property of the girl's parents and could only be redeemed if the boy married the girl.

Wizards were usually held responsible for causing deaths, the failure of crops, long periods of drought and other devilish acts against society. Such wizards, whenever caught or proven, were executed. Proof in such cases was always arbitrary. Part of such proof was the possession of odd objects whose purpose was completely unknown to the people, for example, the placenta of a new born baby or the bones of a dead person.

## The family shrine (*Abila*)

It was built in front of the home and it was identified by particular plants. This shrine had a great degree of sacredness surrounding it. It was not only a resting place for the ancestral spirits but it was also a place where the hunting spears were blessed before and after the hunt. All skulls of the animals which were killed during the hunt were placed at the abila and, except for the very elderly, women were forbidden from changing anything placed at the *abila*.

## Economy

The Langi were originally pastoral and they ate meat and milk mixed with blood. Their economy was non-monetary and they used to barter goats, grains and cattle with the Acholi, the Labwor, the Kumam and later, with the Arabs. As they continued to be pushed towards the shores of Lake Kioga, they discarded their pastoral economy.

Their first food crops were millet (*okama*), and *atunuru ngor* (pigeon peas), *amola* (*hyptis* species) *toke*, *aduru*, *malakwang* (*hibiscus* species) *adura* (*eratocheca sesamoides*) *okwer* (a species of cucumber), *alao* (*crotalaria species*) and *otigo* (*corchorus* species)

Later, the Langi started to grow groundnuts and sweet potatoes which were introduced from Bunyoro during the reign of Kabalega. They also grow and eat simsim and cassava which were introduced by the colonial government in 1911. They used to eat the meat of almost all wild birds and animals except the jackal and the hyena. Another thing they could not eat was *byero* (afterbirth of cows, sheep or goats).

*Farming with oxen*

# The Karimojong

The Karimojong are found in the Kotido and Moroto districts in the northeastern part of Uganda. They are part of the Atekerin-speaking peoples of Uganda. The origins of the word *Karimoja* are quite uncertain but a legend from Teso and Karamoja itself asserts that the two names Iteso and Karimojong were derived during their migrations within Uganda. In their early migrations, the Atekerin peoples are said to have come by way of Karamoja. Those who remained where the Karimojong live today came to be known as the Karimojong. The term is said to have been derived from the phrase: *akarima ajong*; meaning "the old men have got tired"; because the Karimojong did not manage to proceed as far as the other peoples of their stock.

Although the Karimojong have common origins with the Langi and Iteso, some elements of their culture differ greatly from those of the Langi because the Langi became more prone to foreign influences during their migratory cycle. Even among the Karimojong of today, the customs which depicted the mode of life of the traditional stock have slightly, if not greatly, been affected by the forces of change such as intercultural adaptations. Nonetheless, the Karimojong still stand as a distinct group with some elements of their cultural heritage intact.

## Marriage

Before a boy could announce his intention to marry, he had to prove to the elders of the village that he was already a man. In early times, when lions and elephants still teemed across the southern Karamoja plains, the boy had to set out alone armed only with a spear and hunt and kill single handed one of the

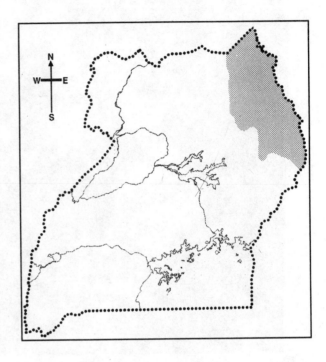

lions or elephants that roamed the plains. The boy would prove the achievement by reporting to the elders at a formal meeting called a *baraza*. He would show the blood on his spear blade and also present the animal's tail. The remaining problem now, would be to find sufficient cattle to pay the bridewealth.

Upon proving his manhood, the boy would be given a bull by his father. The bull was then killed and shared among the boy's male friends and relatives. Besides, the boy would smear himself all over with dung from the entrails of the bull. The boy's hair would then be cut by one of his adult male friends, leaving a tuft at the back known as *input* to which a short string would be tied. From then on, he was considered to have attained marriageable age and with the permission of the elders he could begin to wear ostrich feathers.

The boy's father would then instruct him to look for a girl to marry. No compulsion was

*Karimojong girls with traditional adornments*

look for a girl to marry. No compulsion was brought to bear on either party in a marriage but the father could reject the boy's choice if he deemed the choice unsatisfactory. Sexual contact was a usual prerequisite for the actual marriage and cases were few in which the bridewealth was paid before such a contact had taken place. The boy would make his choice and instruct the father to pay the bridewealth and this marked the beginning of negotiations between the girl's and the boy's families. The first journey of the boy's parents to the girl's home could not be undertaken at the period of the new moon.

When the bridewealth arrangements were finalised, the bride would be brought along with the delegation that came to collect the cows and she would be left at her new home. A delegation from the boy's family would accompany the dowry and on reaching the girl's home, they were received outside the girl's mother's hut. She would spread out hides for all to sit down on whilst she lit a pipe which was handed around and puffed by all in turn, the elders first. Thereafter, the delegation would return home.

When they reached home, the boy would remove the leopard skin and the white ostrich feather he had been wearing. He would not sleep with his bride that night. On the following morning, the boy's mother would take a calabash of cooking butter to the door of the bride's apartment and call for her. She would then put a necklace and a piece of *emuria* grass on the bride and smear the butter all over her, except her legs. She would then remove all the girl's ornaments and dress her like a married woman. The exact attire consisted of a goat-skin hung down behind from the waist, the hairy side outward and a calf skin slung from the shoulders and reaching the knees. The goat-skin had to be well shaped otherwise it could cause shame to the bride among her fellow women when walking or dancing.

After being dressed, the bride and three other girls would go and cut a load of firewood each to give to the boy's mother. That same night, the boy would sleep with his wife and they would continue to do so in the same hut until a child was born. After that, the husband would build a separate hut for that particular wife.

The Karimojong were polygamous. The number of wives a man could marry was only limited by bridewealth obligations. No marriage between relatives was allowed, no matter how remote the degree of consanguinity. Customarily, on arrival at the home of her husband-to-be, the girl was taken through the large kraal entrance and led to her own house. Donning his leopard-skin cloak, his knee bells, headdress and zebra tail, the groom would circle all the village pretending to be a brave animal, tossing his head and swishing his tail. Finally, people would gather in the cattle kraal and the ceremony would be rounded off with a dance.

## Divorce

Normally, if divorce had been agreed upon, the woman would go down on her hands before the husband and he would pour cold water on her back. Thereafter, she could return to her father and the father would repay the bridewealth. When this had been done, the man would return a bull to the woman's father. This bull was killed and all the relatives would join in eating it; even the former husband would take part in the eating. The woman's father and his people would smear the woman with the dung of the entrails to let those concerned understand that she was there and then a free woman.

*Jie man from Karamoja*

If she had not given birth, she would revert to the dressing style of unmarried girls which consisted of a goat-skin covering her buttocks and reaching from the waist to the back of the knees and a pad of cowries covering the front. If however, she had already given birth, she would maintain the dress of a married woman. She could also wear any ornament she liked. A divorced woman could by custom freely remarry.

## Adultery

In the older Karimojong customs, sexual intercourse among unmarried persons was allowed but a pregnancy resulting from such an act was decried. Such a misconduct was atoned for by the payment of thirty goats to the girl's father unless bridewealth was paid and the boy married the girl. But adultery was regarded as the most serious offence rendering the man involved liable to death at the hands of the aggrieved husband. If the adulterer was lucky the offended man could just confiscate all his stock. This penalty was extended to include any stock which the adulterer might come to possess in future until it was felt that the honour of the affected man had been restored. The issue of adultery was in fact a family affair, not a personal one; and the property which was confiscated from the adulterer would be divided up amongst the members of the affected family.

## Birth

When a woman was about to give birth, her female relatives would come to assist. The woman who acted as a midwife would crouch in front and receive the baby. She would wash the baby at once with cold water. The umbilical cord was cut and buried in the cattle enclosure. If the baby was a boy, the cord was cut with *emal* (an arrow used for bleeding cattle); and if a girl, it would be cut with a normal knife. On the day of birth, the mother and her attendants were given food consisting of *choroko* (small peas or beans ground up). They were also given meat and blood from a bull and a heifer. The men could share in the meal but under no circumstances could they enter the hut in which the baby had been born. All the prepared food had to be eaten there and then but no sick person or anyone infected with sores would join the eating.

That same day, the husband would send his wife the skin of a gazelle to be tied by the forelegs behind her back and the hind legs behind her waist in such a fashion as to conceal her breasts. The husband would not enter the mother's house for about twenty days but he could from time to time peer into the hut to inquire about the health of the mother and the child.

On the day when the woman ended the days of confinement, a ritual ceremony was performed. A ram was slaughtered and its skin was prepared for tying the child on the mother's back. The village elder would receive the tongue, a shoulder and the ribs of the ram leaving the remainder to be eaten by the women and the children. A bull or a barren cow would also be killed for the villagers. A few months later, a beer party would be organised. Among the Karimojong, it was considered lucky for a woman to give birth to twins but it was believed that if both of them grew up, either the father or mother would sicken and die.

## Naming

Children were given the names of their ancestors. In fact, to be more exact, the eldest child would get the name of the grandfather. The next would get the name of the grandmother, the third was named after a great aunt or uncle; and so on. This implied in effect that the Karimojong did not have particular names for particular sexes.

Children could also be given other names by the midwives who assisted in their births on account of the conditions prevailing during birth. For instance, a child could be named *Lopero* if it was born at night. However, such names were more often than not, tentatively conferred and acceptance or refusal was said to be demonstrated by the child sucking contentedly or crying. If the mother did not have enough milk to feed the baby, it would be given goat's milk administered from a small gourd shaped like a feeding bottle.

## Death

When a village member died, there was unrestrained weeping. If a woman lost a child through any cause, she would often attempt suicide. Women were known to keep a special cord in their grain baskets for this purpose. It was unusual for a man in Karamoja to attempt suicide; but it was common for women even in the event of loss or failure of crops. Near Latome, there is a stream called "the stream of hanging". By the banks of this stream, it is said that bodies were constantly found hanging from trees.

## Burial

The elder of the village was buried in the centre of the calf or sheep kraal. He was buried with his head pointing to the north because the Karimojong believe that they came from the north. The body was covered with cow dung and soil and then stamped on. Then a large stone would be placed upright on the grave. If an elder died away from the village, his body would be carried home, usually on a donkey. Death and burial ceremonies tended to vary from clan to clan but generally, mourning and weeping would proceed for a couple of days. Among the Karimojong, the *Ng'inga'aricum* clan did not bury their dead. The dead body was usually left outside, preferably at a place where the harvester ants had carried off the seeds and left a bare patch on the ground. The corpse was laid on its side with its head upon a stone, and left there to rot and dry. There were no burials for the lepers and suicide victims.

After burial, the male members would shave the front of their heads while the women would shave off all their hair. All neck ornaments were taken off and the widow would, in addition, remove her earrings. Children and women would also replace their skins with old and tattered ones. In some of the clans, the widow would wear a long skin extending from the chest to the feet and she would also put on her late husband's sandals which she would not take off even if the ground was muddy and even at night when she lay down to sleep. She would also carry her late husband's stick and gourd from which the spout would have been knocked off as a matter of custom.

When the hair had grown again but was still short, the mourners would rub themselves all over with dust to rid themselves of the contamination of the dead. The dead man's contemporaries would then kill his favourite ox and eat it. There were no supplications offered at this ceremony. The dead man's relatives would come and if he had brothers, they would inherit his wives and part of the wealth. But it was not usual among the Karimojong to discuss inheritance until after quite some time. If the man had no brothers, the eldest son would inherit the younger wives but it would take several months before the formal distribution would be done.

Whenever a chief died, he would be buried in the centre of the kraal. The wives and members of the family were usually buried round the sides of or near the entrance of the kraal. Though they tended to have some elements of similarity with the Turkana of Kenya, the Karimojong would not leave the village after someone had died like the Turkana did.

*A young Karimojong man*

## Religion

The Karimojong would not worship for the sake of it. In times of trouble, sickness or misfortune, the clans would gather together at the ancestor's grave with all their children and grand-children and there they would milk the cows, bring out the tobacco and kill an ox. The contents of the ox's stomach were smeared over the people and over the burial stones chanted as follows:

Our father, help us; what shall we do?
Are our cattle to die? Are our children to die?
We have never disobeyed you: oh father, hear us, give us life.

## Rainmaking (*akirriket*)

If rain failed to come at the expected time or when at any moment rain was badly needed, two or three elders would approach the *emurron* (medicine man) with a present of a calabash of milk and impress upon him the necessity of making rain. The emurron would direct them to present a bull of a specified colour, usually black, and then appoint a day for *akirriket* (the rainmaking ceremony). The elders would then look for the appropriate bull, and its owner, as a matter of course, would have to agree to give it away.

On the day of the ceremony, all the elders would gather at the appointed spot. The elders would sit in a semi-circle with the bull in the centre. The other men would group themselves at the opening of the circle where fire was made. Grass was then spread in front of each elder and near the bull. A man was then selected to kill the bull by spearing it in the side. For such a privilege conferred upon him, he had to give the owner of the bull a heifer.

The bull was slaughtered on the grass and the meat would be roasted. The roasted meat was brought before the assembly but it was not distributed immediately. Then the emurron would stand in the centre facing outward and, sticking his naked spear upright in the ground, he would call upon rain to come. It was said that rain would fall instantly or at least within a few days.

The roasted meat was then distributed by two attendants to the elders. The elders would eat and give some bits of meat to the other men around. For his services, the emurron would get a hind leg to himself. He would then cut and divide the other hind leg and distribute it to the elders. Thereafter, all the elders would disperse to their homes.

## The ox of invocation

Customarily, each Karimojong man would keep a special ox among his herd. Each man should simulate acts of bravery by invoking the aid of his special ox. He would do this by calling out the name of the ox while brandishing his spear. If a man killed an enemy or a fierce animal having invoked the aid of his ox, he was entitled to slit the ox's ears. It was believed and feared that an ox might despise a master who had failed to slit its ears.

The oxen of invocation were named according to a list of clan names or on account of colour or the shape of the horns. These oxen were highly esteemed and were valued more than parents, wives, children or other possessions. It was considered very unfortunate for an ox to die before its master. Should it do so, the owner would take off his ornaments and observe many days of mourning. If the master died before the ox, it would be killed to accompany him.

Often, a man could decide to kill his special ox if he realised that it was growing very old. However, only the men belonging to the two elder groups, the *Ng'itukoi* and *Ng'imoru* could be allowed to do such a thing. Such a man would announce his intention to kill the ox.

The representatives of the villages would gather on the ceremonial ground for local and inter-tribal feasts and dances. Customarily, the elders would sit behind the circle of leaves prepared for the occasion. The sticks on which the hind legs of the animal would be placed were laid in the centre before the chief elder.

Therefore, the ox was slaughtered while its owner stood by. He would be dressed in the ceremonial dress of ostrich feathers from head to toe. He would watch but could not himself participate in the slaughter of the ox. Then there would follow dancing and invocation of oxen but as the youths recounted their heroic deeds done in the names of their different oxen, the elders would remain seated. After this there would follow a ceremonial dance which was accompanied by a series of mimed interludes performed by almost everyone present.

As the dancing would be going on, the elders would be given the best pieces of meat. The delegates from the different villages would not go home that day. They would be lodged in the village of the clan to which the owner of the ox belonged. At the end of the celebrations, the revelling and feasts could continue for several days. The owner of the ox would take one new ox in the hope that it would stimulate him to fresh deeds of bravery.

## Economy

The Karimojong were pastoralists by nature and their love for cattle was intense. Cows were regarded as a means of livelihood and for paying bridewealth. Among the Karimojong, the bridewealth was high and it was paid in cows. Brides were very expensive items. Bridewealth ranged from fifty to one hundred heads of cattle. It was due to this and the custom of spear blooding that the Karimojong usually resorted to cattle raiding.

To most of them, spear blooding was necessary when a young boy had passed through what was known as the initiate stage and desired to get married.

## Food

Karimojong food consisted of milk and defibrinated blood. It was usually supplemented with meat, millet, sorghum and beans. When the cows or goats died, they would eat the meat but they would not naturally kill them for food. When they ate meat, they did it thoroughly; the whole carcass save hides, horns and hooves was consumed. The children were usually given milk from the age of six months when breast milk became inadequate.

They would get the blood by bleeding cows. This was done by piercing the jugular vein by shooting an arrow at it. The blood would then be collected in a calabash. It was stirred with a stick until the fibrin separated from it. It was removed and given to dogs during times of plenty but during the dry season, people would cook it and eat it.

The bloody liquid which remained was mixed with an equal volume of milk and the mixture made a meal for a man. This mixture was not cooked in any way. It was simply drunk. In the rainy season when there was enough grass for grazing, this kind of meal was taken daily. However, in the dry season, it was taken only once or twice a week. Millet and maize flour tended to predominate among the rest of the dry season foods.

## Political set-up

The Karimojong were a segmentary society. Leadership was vested in the elders and the clan was the basic unit of political administration. The heads of the different clans constituted the council of elders which was constituted the council of elders which was responsible for administering justice, settling disputes, maintaining law and order, and punishing law breakers.

All the elders occupied a position of political importance in the society. They also performed other important functions connected with rainmaking and tendering sacrifices to

*Karimojong taking their staple food: milk and blood*

# The Iteso

The Iteso live in eastern Uganda in the districts of Soroti and Kumi. Some are in Pallisa and Tororo districts. The political insecurity of the early 1980's caused many Iteso to move as far south as Iganga district. They are part of the Lango group which is said to have come from Abyssinia. By the first half of the 18th century they had settled on the shores of L. Salisbury.

Tradition asserts that the ancestors of the Iteso came from the direction of Abyssinia through Karamoja. Historians have modified this tradition to assert that the Iteso are a Nilo-Hamitic group with similar origins as the Langi, the Karimojong, the Jie and the Kumam.

## Political set-up

The clan was a basic social and political unit. It was administrative and judicial in character. Initially Iteso society was comprised of nine clans. The subsequent clans are said to have broken off from the nine. Each clan had a leader called *Apolon ka Ateker*. He was normally elected from other elders at a merry ceremony known as *Airukorin*. The person selected as Apolon ka Ateker was usually a person of courage, impartiality and wisdom. The actual inauguration ceremony involved opening up a road that had been deliberately blocked for about two weeks. Previously, the Apolon ka Ateker was greatly respected. He acted as an arbitrator in the event of disputes. During the British colonial administration his position was reduced to that of a third grade chief and referred to as *omusalatuo*.

## Settlement of disputes

The clan leader was assisted by a council of elders known as *Airabis* or *Aurianet*. This coun-

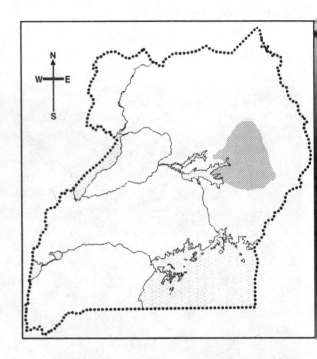

cil dealt with cases like murder and debts. In cases involving murder, compensation could be paid in the form of a girl or a cow. During inter-clan settlements, the elders would come fully armed. In case the other side showed uncompromising behaviour, fighting could easily ensue. After settling a dispute, a ceremony known as *epucit* or *aijuk* was performed whereby a bull was exacted from the offending side and killed, roasted and eaten there and then. This was intended to act as a gesture of renewed co-operation between the two clans. The appropriate compensation in form of a cow or a girl would then be handed over. The girl so given, would have an iron ring put in her ear lobe. If the girl was lacking in beauty, some cows would also be paid to boost her value. After the ceremony and payment of the compensation, it would be assumed that the murder case was sufficiently settled.

*An Iteso traditional dancer*

In the case of a bad debtor, the offender was asked to pay the debt within an agreed period. If he refused or defaulted, he would be caught and tied to a log and left there until his clan rescued him by paying back the debts he owed.

## Military organisation

The age-grades known as *aturio* provided the basis of the military organisation. The war leaders were called *Aruwok* and the army was called the *Ajore*. Before declaring war, the *Amurwok* (fortune teller) would be consulted. If he predicted success, war would be declared after the collective approval of the elders.

## Social set-up

The social system of the Iteso was centred around the clan system and they shared similar cultural elements with the Langi and the Karimojong. Also, due to the influence of the Karimojong. Also, due to the influence of the neighbouring Bantu societies, particularly the Basoga, the Iteso women used to wear barkcloth while the young girls wore *itibire* which were decorated with beads and *arobai*.

## Marriage

Previously, parents could arrange marriage for their children even without their knowledge. However, the boy could directly consult the girl. If the girl consented, she would inform her mother and secretly move away to start staying with the boy. Whenever the girl's clan noticed this development they would complain about the illegal manner in which their daughter was being used. Arrangements would then be made and a date would be fixed on which a delegation from the boy's clan would come to the girl's family for introduction. Arrangements for the payment of bridewealth would be made. In other cases, the boy would approach the girl and tender his wish to marry her. He would then come with a delegation to the girl's family for introduction. The relationship would then be formalised by paying bridewealth. A traditional wedding ceremony would follow.

When all was set and many people had gathered, a table was put in the middle of the gathering. The suitor would put a present on it up. If the girl accepted him, she would pick up the present, amidst cheers and claps. If she did not accept it, she was not willing to get married to him. She would refuse to pick it. This would be the end of any further efforts by the boy to lure her into marriage.

On returning home, the boy and his delegation would inform his parents of whatever had transpired. If the girl had consented, due arrangements would be made to pay the bridewealth. This was settled using sticks to represent the number of cows which were required. All the clan members would gather

for the function. Among the Iteso a child belonged to the whole clan and not to a particular family. On reaching an agreement, another day was set for the girl's family to select the cows. It was fashionable for the girl to go to the boy's home and receive her people as they came to select the cows.

After the cows had been seen and approved, another day was fixed on which the cows would be taken to the girl's home. This would be the same day on which the girl would be escorted to the boy's home to begin her married life. Before entering the compound, the delegation that had brought the cows would ask for a hen to roast and then there would follow a lot of eating, dancing, drinking and merrymaking. Later, an entourage (*mugolen*) would escort the bride to her husband's home. This would be late in the evening or at night. The marching was punctuated by singing and rejoicing. The bride was left at her husband's home with two other girls, to help her get along, as it were. After one month or so, the two girls would also go home and leave the newlyweds to manage their own affairs.

## Birth and naming

There were three types of births among the Iteso: the single child, twins and the spiritual birth. The first two types were considered normal but the spiritual birth was said to be in form of air or water. It was believed that such a child would often manifest itself in a home in the form of a cat or some other animal.

There was no particular formula for naming children. A child could be named according to the circumstances in which it was born or the particular conditions which were experienced by the mother during labour or pregnancy. A child could also be named according to the season to reflect instances like famine, harvest or drought. It could also be named according to the particular day of the week or the time at which it was born; in the morning, during the day or at night. Finally it was common for a child to be named after an ancestor as a sign of commemorating him.

The newborn baby would be initiated into the clan by conducting a ritual ceremony called *etale*. It was after this that the child would be regarded as a full member of the clan. Normally, this ceremony was restricted to the members of the clan but some clans would allow outsiders to participate. The roads and paths leading to the compound where the ceremony was being conducted were lined with thorns in order to prevent outsiders from attending. It was feared that the outsiders might use their evil eyes or perform other devilish acts to undermine the health of the child. Intruders were thus regarded as agents of evil. If caught they were heavily fined or beaten up.

The etale involved a lot of eating and drinking. The food consisted of millet not mixed with cassava and unsalted peas with groundnut paste and oil. Besides, people would also eat *akobokob* (a species of cucumber) and simsim paste. The use of pots was prohibited, so also was the use of tubes for drinking. Only calabashes called *adere* were used for drinking *ajon*. No fighting or quarrels of any sort were allowed and any offenders in this respect were heavily fined in the form of goats and hens. The ceremony acquired a spiritual aspect because it was believed that failure to accomplish it would malign and weaken the child thereby rendering it vulnerable to the wiles of evil doers.

## Death

The Iteso did not regard death as a normal consequence. Death was attributed to ancestral spirits and witchcraft. As soon as a person died a witch doctor would be consulted to diagonose the cause of the death. The corpse was washed in the courtyard and wrapped in *abangut* (barkcloth). Then it was buried. The corpse of a woman was made to lie on its right side while that of a man was laid on its left side. It was customary to bury corpses with certain objects such as needles or razor blades to protect them against cannibals who might use their black magic to extract the corpses from the graves. If the corpse had a needle, for example, it would reply that it was still busy mending its cloth and thus refuse to come out of the grave when invoked by a cannibal.

## Food

The Iteso had a variety of foods. Millet was their staple food. Other varieties included pumpkins, wild berries, groundnuts, peas, beans, meat of both domestic and wild animals, milk, butter and fish. The men did not eat with women. They ate separately, seated on stools, tree stumps or stones. Millet was served on one plate which would be shared communally. The women sat on mats in a circle around the food. It was considered good manners to join the circle whenever one was invited to partake of a meal.

## Religion

The Iteso believed in a supreme being called *Edeke*. However, they were much more involved with ancestral spirits which were believed to cause ill luck if not well attended to. Every family possessed an ancestral shrine where libations were often poured or placed to placate the ancestors. The Iteso were a superstitious society and they believed in witchcraft and wizardry.

It was considered taboo for women to eat chicken. Particular clans had specific taboos, mainly animals they were not permitted to eat. The bush-buck (*ederet*) was taboo to a number of clans.

*Using baskets to catch mudfish in Teso*

*Fishing with spears in Teso*

*An Itesot man transporting fish to the market*

*A human–shaped stool from Teso*

## Utensils and crafts

The women's utensils included baskets, gourds, calabashes, winnowing trays, grinding stones, pots, brooms, pestles and mortars, *ekigo* (ladle for stirring millet) and *eitereria* (the fishing basket). The men's utensils included spears, hoes, clubs, arrows, bows and all the instruments which had to do with brewing and drinking.

## Dances

Whenever a mother gave birth to twins she was styled *toto idwe* (mother of many). Upon that accomplishment, a special type of drum was beaten and the people would gather and dance their best. This involved a lot of eating, drinking and merrymaking.

Another type of dance was known as *Akembe*. It was normally organised by boys who would invite girls to join their company in some generally agreeable place away from homes. It was a get-together dance for boys to spot their future spouses.

Sometimes, when the need arose, a special dance would be held to invoke the ancestors for consultation. A special drum was sounded and the people would dance to an Iteso tune. In the process, some people would become possessed and start communicating to the living, so they say, in the voices of the ancestors. This dance involved shaking rattles. The other dances were general. Some were performed at marriage ceremonies, beer parties, visits and other merrymaking occasions. The dancing instruments included: the *emudiri* and *akong* drums, lutes, *adigidig* and *amagarit*.

*Drinking ajon (millet beer), a popular practice in Teso*

# The Kumam

The Kumam belong to the Atekerin family together with the Langi, the Iteso and the Karimojong. This is the group of people which is often referred to as the Nilo-Hamites. They live in the western areas of Teso and south-east of Lango. In Teso, they are found in the counties of Kaberamaido, Soroti and Serere and, in Lango, in the county of Kioga. Today, they can also be traced in other areas of Uganda particularly in Busoga, Tororo and Buganda. Although they speak a Lwo dialect, their language is not Luo. It is Kumam. The Kumam language is over two-thirds Lwo and one-third Ateso.

## Origin

Historians claim that the Kumam came from the north-east in the direction of Ethiopia from around A.D. 1600. It is further asserted that they derived from people who were originally Ateso speakers and who later learnt Lwo. It is said that due to contact with the Lwo-speaking peoples from around Mt. Otukei and Wila in Karamoja, the Ateso (Dum) speech was abandoned and the Lwo speech was adopted.

They claim that their former name was *leno*. This can be evidenced by such phrases in their language as *yo lango* (path), *pale lango* (home), *yat lango* (medicine) and several others. They have common characteristics with the Iteso and the Lango with respect to birth rituals, certain social customs and hunting practices.

The Karimojong use the same word *Kumama* when referring to the Iteso, the Langi and the Kumam. It is generally agreed that *Kumam* is derived from the Lango word *Akum*, meaning those people of the former Teso district who included the Iteso and some Langi. The Kumam are also referred to as the

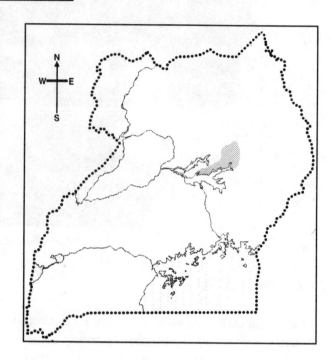

*Ikokolemo. Ikoku* is an Iteso word meaning "child" while *elem* is a Luo word meaning headdress. This means that the Kumam are a mixture of Luo and the Atekerin possibly as a result of intermarriages between the Luo and Ateker-speaking peoples. As the Luo settled in northern Uganda, they came into contact with the Atekerin peoples who were also at the same time moving from the northeast and founding settlements in northeastern Uganda. The fact that their language is half Lwo and half Ateker, lends some truth to this presupposition. Another legend talks of a boy who stole *elem* and fled somewhere with it and his descendants became the Kumam.

## Political set-up

The Kumam had a loose political structure under clan leaders known as *Wegi Atekerin*.

Other people of importance in the society were *Wegi Ikodeta Cel* (leaders of dancing groups), and leaders of *Asonya* homes, *Wengi Cel*. The *Wengi Cel* were in most cases *Dogolan* or *Odonge Ikekoros* (heads of part of a clan descending from one man). These clan leaders were responsible for the maintenance of law and order as well as general administration. They arbitrated in matters of politics and social affairs.

## Social set-up

Their social system had elements of both Langi and Iteso cultures. However, they were nearer to the Iteso than to the Langi. This was because the Langi were so much subjected to Luo influence that they lost most of their original culture.

## Marriage

Previously, the parents would arrange marriages for their children. Girls of a tender age could be betrothed to boys. In effect the young girl would become wife of the respective boy but she would wait to be officially handed over when she came of age. In some cases, the young girls so betrothed would be taken to the boy's home to grow up there. When she came of age, a ceremony would be organised to

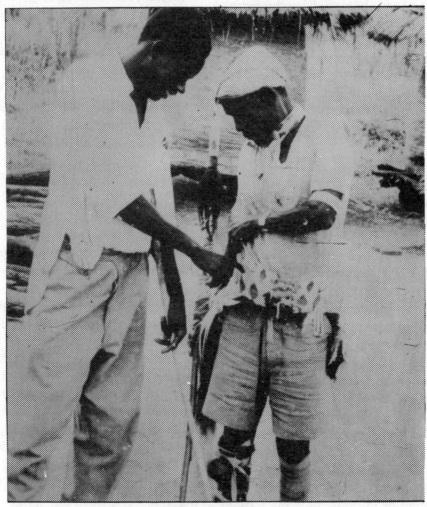

*A Kumam dancer*

formalise the relationship. With time however, the system changed. A boy would look for a girl and without the consent of her parents, sneak with her to his home at night.

After a week or so, the girl's relatives would begin to look for her. Obviously they had some prior knowledge of her whereabouts. On discovery, a fine would be exacted from the boy. Arrangements would be made to settle the bridewealth and the marriage would be formalised.

If the girl's parents did not trace her whereabouts it was normal for her to go home and tell them what had happened to her. Then due arrangements would be made to obtain the fine and bridewealth from her husband. The normal procedure was that the girl's relatives would go to the boy's home where the bridewealth would be negotiated. The cows could be taken that same day. Formerly, the number of cows which was paid was very large. It ranged between twelve to fifteen head of cattle. The exact number depended on how hard-working the girl was.

## Birth

Whenever a woman was pregnant, she was not supposed to eat the intestines of any animal. After giving birth, a feast was organised. If the new-born child was a boy, it was given a spear and if a girl, it was given a calabash. This ritual of giving a spear or a calabash to the new-born was designed, so they say, to protect the child against bad omens. The name given to the child would reflect the experiences surrounding its birth or the experiences of the parents who named it. For instance, if one's children had been dying young, a new-born child was named *Alobo* if it was a girl or *Lobolo* if it was a boy. The umbilical cord and the placenta were buried in the house under a big pot previously used for keeping water. The purpose of this was to put them out of the reach of wizards and other ill-wishers who might use them to affect the health of the child or to undermine the fertility of the mother.

Twins were considered good. Special rituals were performed after their birth. When twins were born, special green vegetables were prepared and the in-laws from the mother's side were invited. A feast would be organised in which there would be a lot of eating and dancing. The ritual ceremony was intended to initiate the twins into the society.

## Death

The Kumam did not believe in such a thing as natural death. Every death was attributed to witchcraft. When one died, there was a lot of weeping and wailing. Burial would wait until all the relatives of the deceased had gathered. Mourning could go on for a week for both men and women. Although they do not appear to have believed in eternal life, they believed that the spirits of the dead did not die. They had power to inflict harm on the living. For this reason the family had a shrine for the ancestral spirits. Here they were fed and rested during their wanderings and visits to the family. In the event of sickness or before going on a hunt or a long journey, one would pass by his ancestors' shrine to ask for health and good fortune.

## Economy

The traditions of the Kumam indicate that they were originally pastoralists. They reared cattle, sheep, goats and chickens. Today they are partly pastoral and partly agricultural. Their staple food crops are *kal* (millet), *bel* (sorghum), *kat* (potatoes) with beans and peas as common sauce. Land was communally owned by the clan. Any member of the clan was fully entitled to use it. Women and children did not own land. The women owned utensils which included *agulu* (big pots), *tabo* (small pots), *itany* (plates made from clay) as well as a variety of baskets and mats.

The Kumam were prone to the influence of the Luo. The Kumam language has a high percentage of Lwo words.

# The Kakwa

The Kakwa live in the extreme northwest of Uganda. They occupy the Koboko county of Arua district. Ethnically, the Kakwa are Plain Nilotes, which means that they are of Kushitic descent.

## Origins

There are two main traditions concerning the origins of the Kakwa. One piece of tradition asserts that the ancestor of the Kakwa of Uganda was Yeki. He is said to have migrated from Karobe Hill, Southern Sudan and settled on Mt. Liru in Koboko. Here, Yeki is said to have produced seven sons one of whom was fond of biting his brothers. For this reason, Yeki is said to have nicknamed him *Kakwan ji*, meaning biter. The descendants of Yeki are said to have adapted the plural term and called themselves *Kakwa*.

The second tradition claims that the Kakwa were originally known as *Kui*. The Kui are said to have been fierce fighters who inflicted heavy losses on their enemies. For this reason, the Kui are said to have nicknamed themselves *Kakwa* because their fierce attacks were like the bite of a tooth. The majority of the Kakwa in Koboko cling firmly to this tradition.

Virtually all the Kakwa clans in the whole of Koboko, part of Maracha and Aringa trace their origin to Loloyi but none of them can tell what or where exactly Loloyi is. By linguistic connection, the Kakwa can be traced to the Bari of southern Sudan. Indeed the Kakwa still believe that they have connections with the Kuku, Mundari, Nyangwar, Pojuru and even the Karimojong.

The Koboko tradition claims that the first Kakwa ancestors came from the direction of

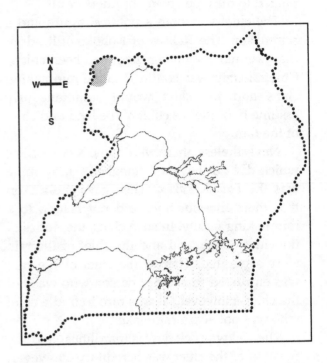

Ethiopia. This tradition does not state, however, the point at which the Kakwa separated from the Bari. The general conjecture is that they split in the Bari country east of the Nile. Given that they are Plain Nilotes like the Iteso and the Karimojong, they might have separated from the Bari at Kapoeta.

## Social and political set-up

The political institutions of the Kakwa were segmentary. They had no centralised system of government and the clan was the basic social and political unit. Each clan was politically independent of others and it enjoyed sufficient traditional loyalty.

At the head of each clan, there was a chief known as the *Matter*. Other clans referred to the chief as the *Buratyo*; and others, *Ba Ambogo*. The highest political officer was the chief and immediately below him were the clan elders known as *Temejik*. The Temejik were more often than not, heads of sub-clans and were related to the chief, being brothers or uncles.

The chief was both a political figure and a rainmaker. The Kakwa of Koboko still admit that rainmakers among them had been chiefs. Chieftainship was confined to the rainmaking clans and the chief would simultaneously assume two titles as chief of the land and chief of the rain.

Nevertheless, there were some Kakwa clans which did not have a rainmaker. An example was the *Ludara Kakwa*. They gave the reason that their ancestor Solo, did not belong to a rainmaking family. In such clans, the duties of the chief of the land and the chief of the rain were separated. That of the chief of the rain was entrusted to another person who was not the chief. However, it was rare to find a chief who was not also a rainmaker.

The Kakwa society was matrilineal and the position of the chief was hereditary. However, among the non-rainmaking clans, the chief's office was not hereditary. Clans without rainmakers could borrow them from other clans and a borrowed rainmaker did not have political influence. He would instead be paid for his services.

## Clientship

There were no distinct classes among the Kakwa but the society contained upper and lower people. The lower people constituted the house servants, cattle herders, and young children.

If an upper-class person looked after such dependents well, they would remain with him even after they married. However, if a client was treated in a hostile manner which made him look subservient, such a client would leave and look for another master. A client would normally leave and go somewhere else if he was referred to as *monyatio* meaning "stranger in the home". Whenever a client attained marriageable age, he would have his bridewealth paid for him by his master. Thereafter, he would become part of the family.

## Choosing and installing a chief

Before a person could assume chieftainship, he had to perform some form of traditional ritual. Normally a chief had a secret bead which was passed down to him by his predecessors. The chief would often drop the bead in food without the knowledge of his sons and invite them to eat. The one who discovered the bead and gave it to his father would become the future successor. From then on his father would make him carry his chiefly stick and stool wherever he went. He was further required to observe carefully what his father was doing in order to become acquainted with his future responsibilities. The elders had the powers to reject such a nominee if it was widely known that he was irresponsible. There were other ways of selecting a successor to chieftainship but this one tended to be the commonest.

If a chief had no sons, his closest relative would succeed him. If a chief died leaving a young son, a regent would be appointed to act in his place until the child came of age. Such a case occurred in Media in the late 1890's. Chief Bongo died and his infant son Baba became the chief-elect. Meanwhile, his nephew, Ali Kenyi was appointed regent. Baba was unfortunate, however, because before he could assume his office effectively, the Belgians came. Ali Kenyi collaborated with them and retained the chair.

During the installation of the chief, all the clan members would gather at the chiefly house known as *Kadina Mata*. They would bring food and beer and it was customary that the elders would sit alone and invoke the ancestral blessings to enable the new chief to lead his people in peace and prosperity. Then there would follow dancing and rejoicing.

## Role of the chief

The chief had to protect the hunting grounds of the clan against other clans and to advise his clan to prevent its cattle from grazing on the crops of other clans. It was his duty to shift his people away in time of danger and to negotiate for peace in the event of external aggression and defeat. Besides, he acted as an adviser to the council of elders. If he acted in his capacity as a rainmaker, he did not need advice from the elders. This was due to the belief that the power to make rain and perform fertility rites could not be possessed by a common man, elderly though he might be.

## Military

The chief had no standing army. However, each chieftainship had a military leader known as the *Jokwe*. Before mobilising for war, the chief and the *Jokwe* would consult the elders and a ritual ceremony would be performed to seek communication from the clan's ancestors about the military strength of the enemy clan.

The ritual consisted of drawing a circle on the ground and then tying a chicken to the centre of it. The circumference of the circle would be labelled alternately with signs of either victory or defeat. The chicken in the centre of the circle would then be slaughtered. If it died near 'defeat', the chief would advise the entire clan not to go to war. He would proceed to negotiate for peace with the head of the enemy clan. If, however, the chicken died near 'victory', the clan had to go to war, no matter how weak it was, because it was believed that the ancestral spirits would give

them support and the strength to win.

In certain cases such as among the *Leiko*, the women would accompany their husbands to war. It is said that such women were not assailed during the war due to the belief that if a man killed a woman during war, the ancestors would not like it and he would therefore fall victim to his enemies much earlier than expected. The purpose of taking women to battles was for them to yell and encourage their husbands. They would also remove the casualties and the dead and hide them until the battle was over.

## Judicial system

Disputes were settled by the clan elders. The most serious of the cases would be referred to the chief. Women and children would not participate in passing judgement. However, unlike the Lugbara who could not allow women and children to linger near the court, the Kakwa allowed them to attend. They were required to sit down and listen but they were not expected to talk except if they were testifying as witnesses.

Some serious cases were often difficult to judge. Serious cases included murder and adultery. If a man was caught committing adultery, he would be killed outright and no one would raise a case against the murderer. Similarly, there was no time for judging a thief. He would be killed as they said, "in the manner foxes are killed" something similar to "mob justice". The murder of a person from another clan would bring warfare between clans and the murdered person was not mourned until sufficient revenge had been effected.

If one killed a clansman, revenge was not approved of. The murderer would pay compensation of a cow or two. People often confessed frankly in the form: "I killed a, b, c, because of x, y, z". If the accused denied the charges, two tests would be carried out to prove him guilty or not guilty. In cases involving witchcraft or poisoning, once the accused pleaded not guilty, the following procedures would be undertaken:

If a woman was accused of having poisoned her husband and she denied it, she would be taken to the stream to prove her innocence. The woman's clansmen and the relatives of the husband would also come to the stream. The woman would then be fed on *jja* or *kuru* (wild plant seeds) and asked to drink plenty of water.

If she was innocent, she was expected to vomit all the water. But if indeed she had poisoned the husband, she would not vomit anything and it was said that her stomach would begin to swell. At that point, she would be killed by the relatives of the husband while her own clansmen looked on. If, however, she vomited the water, her relatives would come to her defence and if she was not compensated for this abuse, war could easily ensue between the two clans. The payment of a bull or a cow by the husband's relatives would restore the woman's reputation and bring things to order once again.

If a couple was caught having sex outside marriage, the boy would be held hostage until his people paid a ransom, usually a cow or four goats in lieu. Quite often, too, the boy would be forced to marry the girl. These were simple cases which could not lead to war between different clans.

## Economy

The economy of the Kakwa was mainly subsistence agriculture but some families also practise mixed farming. They kept cattle, goats and sheep besides agriculture. Millet has always been their principal food crop followed by sorghum and a type of bean called *burusu*. These were the staple foods of the Kakwa. They have been supplemented by pawpaws, maize and cassava. Cassava is said to have come with the advent of the Belgians and the intrusion of the Logo, an ethnic group from Zaire. Pawpaws are said to have been introduced by the British.

Millet, sorghum and *burusu* were traditionally sown in one large field dug on a communal basis, known as *vya* or *litika*. Women figured less prominently in the economy of the Kakwa. Men dug the fields, sowed the seeds, tended the animals, built and repaired the houses. Women would remove the rubbish from the cultivated fields, weed and harvest the crops. Besides, they would also clean and store the crops away in granaries.

The women engaged actively in basket weaving, salt making and pottery. Salt was made from indigenous plants known as *morobu* and *bukuli*. These plants would be burnt and then the ashes were put in a container with many holes at the bottom; water would be poured on the ashes. The salty liquid would filter through the holes and out into another container at the bottom.

The *Nyangilia* clan specialised in iron smelting, making spears, knives, hoes and a variety of other iron implements. Wealth among the Kakwa was measured in terms of "how many granaries full of foodstuffs" one had in one's compound and the number of he livestock in one's kraal. In the event of famine, and this was common, people would migrate to another area where there was plenty of food.

# - 5 -

# Madi-Moru Group

Besides those in Uganda, this group of people are found in southern Sudan, north-eastern Zaire, and the Central African Republic. In Uganda it includes the Lugbara, the Madi, the Metu, the Okebu and the Lendu. They all trace their origins from southern Sudan but their customs and cultures differ significantly.

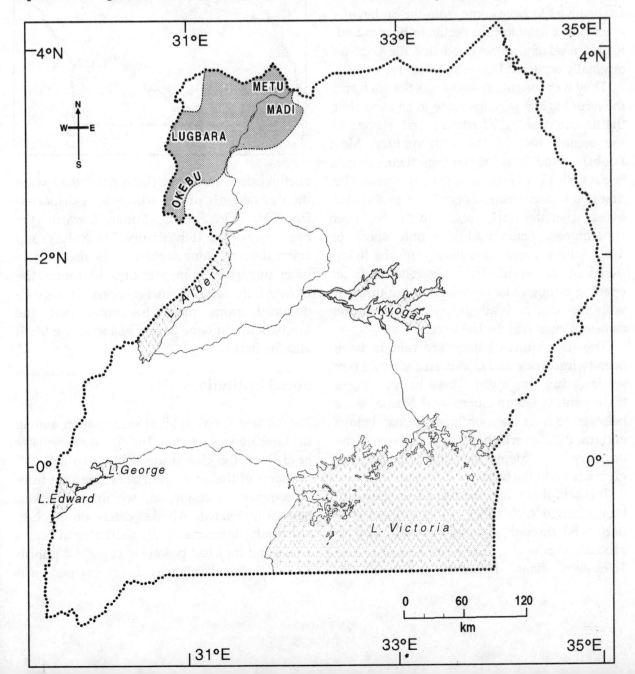

# The Lugbara

The Lugbara constitute the largest ethnic group in West Nile.

## Origins

The Lugbara are a Sudanic-speaking people and their language is one of the eastern Sudanic languages of the Madi, the Lugbara, the Keriko, the Logo and the Avukaya. They are believed to have come from the Sudan at a place called Rajaf in Juba region or Baar in Bari. Recent research has revealed that the Lugbara originally occupied Loloyi and Baar regions.

They were originally known as the *Madi* and the term *Lugbara* perhaps came to be used after the intrusion of the Khartoum Arab slavers in the second half of the 19th century. Most Lugbara traditions regarding their origins begin with God's creation of the universe. The first two human beings *Gboro-Gboro* (male) and *Meme* (female) are said to have been superhuman. Some traditions only speak of *Meme* whose womb God filled with the living things of the world. Then a gazelle made an opening through Meme's womb by rupturing it with its hoof and all the worldly creatures came out; man was the last to come out.

The first human beings are said to have been twins: *Arube* and *O'duu*. Arube was a boy while O'duu was a girl. These twins, unlike their parents Gboro-Gboro and Meme, were believed to have been ordinary human beings and tradition asserts that they were born in the ordinary way. Meme died immediately after giving birth to the twins.

It is said that when these children grew up, they married each other and produced children who through generations multiplied to produce the *Jokodra, Lebenyere, Mutalema* and *Telebenyere* clans. However, most of the

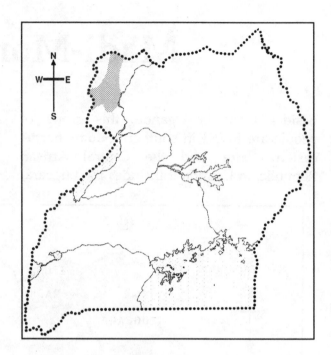

northwestern Lugbara, claim that they were the descendants of *Jaki* whose sons dispersed from Mt. Liru in the Sudan towards the beginning of the 18th century. The *Rubu* group claim descent from *Aroba* who is also said to have migrated from Mt. Liru to found the *Otrabu-Rubu* and *Rubu-Yia* clans. It can be deduced from these traditions that the Lugbara might have been a fusion of the Madi and the Bari.

## Social institutions

The highest social political organisation among the Lugbara was the clan. The clan was normally headed by the clan leader called the *Opi*. All members of the same clan claimed descent from a common ancestor to whom they were paternally related. All the elders of the clan exercised influence over political and social affairs and they had powers to curse and punish any of their subordinates. Every married man had authority over his wives and children and even after his sons had married, he still had power over them and their children.

The Lugbara had a clientage system called *Amadingo* whereby the poor or the destitute would be looked after by the rich. Such clients were treated as members of the family and they could be given land if they wished to stay. Bridewealth would even be paid for them by their hosts if they wished to marry during their clientage.

## Birth

Whenever a child was born, the first thing to be done was the ritual of cutting off the umbilical cord. If the baby was a boy, the acting midwife was required to cut the cord in four strokes. If the baby was a girl, the cord was cut in three strokes. In traditional Lugbara, the numbers four and three symbolise men and women respectively.

After giving birth the mother would stay in confinement for three or four days depending on the sex of the child. Besides, she was required to abstain from eating certain foods and could only receive a few visitors because some might have evil intentions and might do harm to the health of the child or even cause its death. The ritual of confinement was followed by the festivities that ended with the naming of the child. The name given portrayed some memorable experience when the child was still unborn. For example, if the child was born during famine, it would be named *Abiriga*.

## Initiation

During puberty, both girls and boys underwent two important rituals of tribal identification. These were face tattooing and the extraction of six frontal teeth from the lower jaw. This was intended both as a way of decoration and as an in initiation into adulthood. These two experiences were said to be very painful albeit compulsory. Anybody who was overdue for these operations would still be called a child. No one would aspire to marry unless he or she had gone through initiation.

## Marriage

In the very distant past, at a time when tribal warfare characterised Lugbara society, courtship is said to have been impossible. In those days, parents used to arrange marriages for their children. Marriage reservations could be made by the parents even when the children were of a tender age.

When warfare subsided considerably, courtship became possible. The boy's father would transfer bridewealth to the girl's home and thereafter, the couple was customarily married. Divorce was rare indeed. It could only occur if the woman failed to have children or if she was found in possession of poisonous charms or any other substance that could be used to kill people.

## Burial

The burial of a chief differed considerably from that of ordinary men. After the announcement of a chief's death, no one was allowed to wail because it was feared that if one wailed before burial, the corpse might turn into a lion or a leopard and attack people. Therefore, prior to the chief's burial, mourners would weep quietly.

A bull was slaughtered for the mourners and its hide was used to wrap the corpse. The burial was in the middle of the night and the body would be placed in the grave with the head pointed northwards towards Mt. Liru where the Lugbara believed they originated. After burial, a sorrowful song would be sung and the mourners would wail as they danced.

*Traditional costumes of the Lugbara*

A barkcloth tree (*laru*) would be planted on the grave. Food could be served during part of the mourning. The paternal relatives of the late *Opi* (chief) would give *avuti* (death duty in the form of a bull) to the chief's maternal relatives.

The burial procedure for ordinary people was similar to that for a chief except that in the event of the death of an ordinary person, mourners were allowed to wail immediately after the death without any fear that the corpse might turn into a lion or a leopard. Besides, the laru was not usually planted on the grave. At all burials, the *adi* (traditional history) of the deceased was recounted and funeral dances were compulsory.

## Avuti

Customarily, an individual was affectionately treated by his mother's relatives who referred to him as *ama ezaapi* (our daughter). He or she referred to them in turn as *adropika* (my uncles). It was the custom that upon an individual's death the maternal clan demanded a death duty in the form of a bull called *avuti* (the corpse bull). It would often generate a mock or real fight if this demand was not granted.

## Political set-up

The political set-up of the Lugbara was segmentary. The most important figure was a chief called *Ozoo-Opi*. He sometimes had both political and rainmaking powers. But in some cases, the Ozo-Opi did not posess rainmaking powers. In such an event, another individual was entrusted with the powers of rainmaking. Such an individual was called the *Ozoo-ei*. The Ozoo-Opi was the chief custodian of the clan's property. In any case, harvesting could not be done without the blessing of the *Opi*. It was his duty to offer new harvests to the gods and he had to taste the produce before the producers could taste them.

In the event of a clan ceremonial feast, he officially opened it by starting to eat before anybody else. He was given the most delicious meat which always included a piece of liver. The Opi rarely offered sacrifices to the ancestors although their power to lead was believed to be derived from the ancestors. They had, however, the duty of offering sacrifices to the god of the clan.

Custom demanded that an Opi should be able to recount the *adi* (testimonies) during funeral rites, serious illness and major social gatherings like marriage ceremonies. The prospective Opi learnt the adi by observation. The actual practice of recounting the adi was solemn. The Opi would stand up and narrate the history of the clan to stress their oneness. Then he would proceed to recount the background of the occasion for which the adi was being recounted. He would symbolically move forward and backwards while shooting an arrow upwards at each stop. If he happened to forget a point, or got mixed up during the process, it was normal and acceptable for another elder to correct him. Usually the adi would be followed by the settlement of the issue at hand.

## Succession of an Opi

Among Lugbara, succession of an *Opi* was a peaceful affair. The date of the succession was a very honourable occasion and it was attended by all the notables of the clan. This occasion was punctuated with a lot of beer and food. Amidst all this, the most senior Opi within the lineage presented the new Opi with an *anderiku* (a chiefly stool which was sometimes simply referred to as *Opi Agua*). After the new Opi had sat on the stool, he was presented with the rest of the chiefly regalia namely, a spear, a bow and arrows, and a bracelet. Then a congregation of lineage chiefs would formally brief the new Opi on the qualities and rules of conduct which would be expected of him as a leader and alert him to the heavy responsibility he would have to shoulder.

## Judicial system

Any affairs which affected the clan were handled by the lineage and clan heads. Normally, minor offences would be settled by the lineage heads but serious ones required the clan heads. Examples of such serious cases included killing a relative, adultery, unpaid loans and the more serious forms of wizardry, witchcraft and sorcery.

The lineage court comprised all the family

heads and it was presided over by the lineage head. The clan court was a higher court comprising all the lineage heads who often co-opted other notables and some wealthy men if they deemed it appropriate.

Court proceedings usually took place under a big tree in the compound and trials were conducted in privacy. As a matter of fact, women and children were not allowed to linger around the area unless they were called upon as witnesses. In an intra-clan affair, a murderer was fined a bull or a cow. For the murder of a man, one was fined a bull, and for the murder of a woman one was fined a cow. In cases involving adultery, it was fashionable to give a bull to the affected husband. Incest was also abhorred and in case it took place, the male relative of the girl was fined a sheep which was slaughtered and eaten by the family to cleanse the sin.

Inter-clan cases were more serious than intra-clan ones. An inter-clan adultery case, for instance, was serious enough to require capital punishment. If caught red-handed, the man would be killed or if he was very lucky, he would simply have his sexual organs maimed. In cases involving fornication, the boy would be held as ransom until he agreed to marry the girl or paid an appropriate fine. Failure to comply would also lead to the maiming of his sexual organs. Unsettled loans would also lead to war between clans.

## Economy

The Lugbara were agriculturalists. They claim in their traditions that they had once owned a lot of cattle which were decimated by rinderpest. During the period of their early migration, they brought with them simple possessions such as sheep, goats, millet and sorghum. They also got food by hunting buffaloes, bush buck, antelopes, rabbits, squirrels and several other animals. In addition, they also carried out fishing and trapped a variety of birds. Both indigenous and migratory grasshoppers were caught and eaten. The roots and fruits of some wild plants were also gathered.

## Property ownership

### Land

The land among the Lugbara was categorised into virgin land, fallow land and land under cultivation. All land within a clan was communally owned and at least theoretically individuals could lay claim to any part of virgin land. The same applied to the fallow land but in this case the consent of the former owner was sought before carrying out any cultivation on it.

### Cattle

Cattle served the needs of the family which owned them. However, theoretically, they were said to belong to the whole clan and the Opi in particular as the chief custodian. The wealthy people, *Barukuza*, had a lot of food, cattle and many wives. For this reason, they wielded much power and influence next to the Opi.

A married woman could not claim independent ownership of property. This was because she was customarily regarded as the husband's property and all that she had was, as a matter of course, his possession. A woman could only control food. Here she was free and she could even deliberately starve her husband and he would not put up a fight.

Children, like women, were not allowed independent ownership of property. The only exception in this case was a boy of marriageable age. If his father died he would automatically claim his father's property as there would be no need for it to taken care of by the lineage or clan heads or the Opi.

### Handicraft

Women produced various articles of handicraft including various types of baskets and pots. The most common were *ivua* (food basket), *kuta* (food cover), *kubi* (sauce pot) and *ajiko* (pot for preparing millet flour). The Lugbara also did some iron smelting and the *ondoo* (clever ones) made iron implements for the rest of the population. There were also among the Lugbara, another ethnic group known as the *Okebu* who specialised in iron smelting.

# The Madi

The Madi live in Moyo district in the extreme north bordering the Sudan. They are Sudanic in language and their origin could be traced to Bari in southern Sudan.

## Birth

One thing that tended to puzzle the Madi was the mystery of birth. All their beliefs were based on reproduction. The term they used for the supreme being who was responsible for births was *Rabanga*. In addition to being a spirit, Rabanga was also regarded as the earth in the sense of "Mother Earth". One old man explained this concept in the following statement:

We see all plants are born from the earth and if the earth cannot make a woman fertile, how does she conceive?

Rabanga was also believed to have created everything.

## Twins

Among the Madi, the birth of twins was believed to be an ill-omen and it was attributed to Rabanga. Twins were regarded as mysterious creatures and in fact the elder of the twins was named *Ejaiya* meaning "take him to the bush" and the younger *Rabanga*.

After the birth of twins, the father and the family of the mother would each bring a sheep to be eaten by the parents of the twins together with the woman who had looked after the twins' mother during the period of confinement. This ceremony was called *Lati*.

The mother's family was required to produce another sheep which would be tied on a bed-like structure made of sticks at the

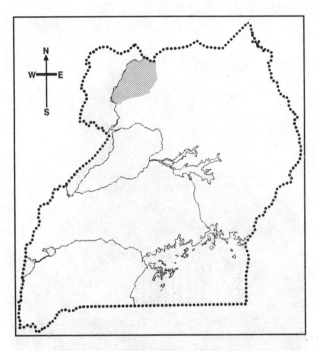

side of the mother's hut every morning and evening. The sheep was allowed to live a normal life with the rest of the sheep apart from mornings and evenings when it was put on the bed. When it gave birth, it was killed and offered as a sacrifice for the well-being of the parents of the twins. The special bed made of sticks on which the sheep was regularly put, was called *Rabanga* and the sheep itself was known as *Rabanga-Bilo*.

## Religion

The whole life of the Madi was centred on the belief that their ancestors survived after death as spirits known as *ori*. They believed that the ori could intervene directly in human affairs. They attributed every misfortune to the anger of such and such a spirit and in the event of any misfortune or sickness, they would immediately consult an *odzo* or *odzogo* (witchdoctor) to find out which ancestor was

*A Madi headdress*

centres. With only two exceptions, rain could be made by the rainmaker by using a special set of stones which were usually white in colour. These "rain stones", as they were called were believed to come with rain from the sky and they could be categorised into "male" and "female" stones. The male stones were conical with fairly sharp points while the female ones would be either round or conical but perhaps without sharp points. Actually, some female stones looked exactly like male ones but the rainmaker could tell which was which without any difficulty.

When "rain stones" were discovered, they were immediately reported to the chief. In the event of thunder or lightning, it is said, the "rain stones" would jump about. They were kept in special pots and they could not be looked at without the permission of the chief or the rainmaker, otherwise they could easily strike the insolent viewer with impotence.

If rain failed to come, people would ask the rainmaker to assist. The ceremony of making rain was completely preserve of the rain maker. The stones were smeared with fat or oil and supplications were made to Rabanga and to the former chiefs. Then the offertory food was eaten and the stones would be placed in a little water. The rainmaker would take the offertory food (*mtami, wimbi* and beans) together with shea-butter nut oil into the hut where the "rain stones" were kept. Then he would put a clay pot on a wooden basin, remove the "rain stones" from their pot, wash them and, calling upon the spirits of the dead chiefs and Rabanga to bring rain, he would put them in a bowl in which they were anointed with a little oil.

The rainmaker's and the chief's principal wives, who were the only people supposed to be present at the ceremony, would cook the beans in the oil and brew beer from the mtami and wimbi. From the remainder of the wimbi, millet

behind the existing ordeal. After that, sacrifices were offered to the particular spirit in order to avert its malign influence on the living. The powerful families among the Madi were believed to have powerful ancestral spirits to help them. The whole paraphernalia of the spirits of the dead was known as *babu-garee*.

## Rainmaking

Within the whole of the Madi community, there were as many as forty-five rainmaking

*Madi musicians*

bread would also be made. This food was eaten by the rainmaker and the two principal women who prepared it. The "rain stones" were then placed in their pot with sufficient water which would be neither too much nor too little. The rainmaker and the two women would neither leave the hut nor eat any other food during the whole day. Rain was expected to fall on that day.

If rain failed to come, an *odzo* would be consulted or, alteratively, the rainmaker would extend the rainmaking ceremony to involve the killing and eating of a sheep. Unless there was something really unnatural, rain was expected to come. If there was too much rain, the rainmaker would pick a branch of a bush called *erewa*, smear it with red ochre and put it in the roof of the hut where the "rain stones" were kept.

It is said that only two clans among the Madi could cause rain to fall without using "rain stones". Their elders would meet at their place of worship and ask Rabanga to bring rain by just praying to him.

## Political set-up

The political set-up of the Madi was closely interwoven with their religious beliefs. They were organized in chiefdoms and each chiefdom was headed by a hereditary chief known as the *Opi*. The Opi exercised both political and religious powers. He was respected not only as a political figure but also as the centre of the collective influence of the former chiefs.

Other people of political and indeed religious importance in Madi society apart from the chiefs were the rainmakers and the *vudipi*. The vudipi exercised an important influence over the land. The chiefs, the rainmakers and the vudipi were all believed to descend from a line of ancestors who performed the same functions. They were also believed to retain similar powers even after they had died. There was a hierarchy of spirits corresponding exactly to the hierarchy of authority as it existed in the society.

*Calabash music from Madi*

## Judicial system

In cases where one pleaded innocent to accusations of stealing or adultery, the witch doctor was consulted. The witch doctor would take a handful of spear grass and order the accuser and the accused to hold each end of the grass. The witch doctor would then cut the spear grass with an arrow. Whoever was guilty would fall sick and the truth would establish itself through the consequences. The guilty one was usually cleansed in the following way:

He would pay a sheep which would be slaughtered. The blood and dung from. the sheep's intestines were smeared on the back of the hands of both the accuser and the accused. Some blood and dung was also smeared on their chests. Their legs were then tied with the sheep's skin and the elders of the two families concerned would eat the meat of the sheep as an act of reconciliation.

In cases involving poisoning, the witch doctor would heat a spear and touch the thigh of the accused with the hot end of the spear. If a weal appeared, then the accused would have been proved guilty and he would be immediately speared to death. It seems automatic that if one was touched with a heated spear on the thigh, a weal would definitely occur. There are stories, however, that cases are known where it did not.

## Superstitions

If a man was going on a journey and he met or saw a rabbit, a bush-buck, or a wild pig, he would turn back and consult a witch doctor to find out what to do before he set off again.

If an owl hooted while perched on one's house or if a man met a certain snake or a leopard, then someone in the family would die.

If a jackal barked inside one's compound, the occupants would at once move to a new site in the belief that the old home was cursed.

There was also a belief that some people had the power to turn into leopards or to speak to leopards and use them for evil deeds.

## Economy

The Madi were settled agriculturalists. Their main crops were *mtami*, *wimbi* and a variety of beans and shea-butternut. Their means of exchange was through the barter system and they are known to have carried out lucrative trade with their neighbours.

In addition, they tended sheep, goats, cattle and chickens. Their general economic structure, like that of most pre-colonial Ugandan societies, was mainly subsistence.

The Metu people are a sub-section of the Madi. They live in the steep and rocky area to the west of Mt. Otze in West Madi. They divide themselves into the higher Metu known as the *Meturu* and the lower Metu known as the *Metuli*.

# The Metu

The Metu were lovers of beauty. They used to smear themselves with a type of red earth known in their language as *era*. They mixed it with simsim oil, shea-butter or castor oil. Mothers and their newborn babies would be completely smeared so as to make them a glistening tomato colour.

Era needs some further mention because it was used in a variety of ways among the Metu. It was used for adornment and in preparation for dances and other great ceremonies, it was smeared on the head. It was also used as a dressing for wounds and ulcers and for general purpose hygiene. With castor oil as a base, it was used as a cure for scabies. Era was used in clearing and polishing the women's head girdles in preparation for big social events.

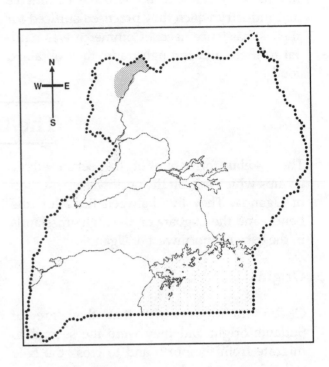

## *Kore* dance

The most important dance among the Metu was the *kore*. Unlike most Madi dances, the kore dance had characteristics of the *kuku* dances. The actual dance took the following pattern:

The men would form a wide circle and dance in a rhythmic tramp, beating time with two pieces of *pinyi* (black wood). The centre of the circle was left clear to be occupied by the principal dancers. The principal dancers were usually men but often a single girl would be chosen because of her attractiveness. The girl would dance solo, swinging her arms in front and backwards. She then chose a particular part of the circle towards which she would dance with her face averted. On reaching that part of the circle, she would dance a little and retreat to the centre, followed by four or five young men. They would dance round her for a few minutes and then return to their former positions to give room for others to dance around her.

## Dwellings

The Metu used to live in very nice huts made of cane basketwork and circular walls. The roof of the hut was made in such a way that it could be lifted off and re-used to construct another hut if the owner deemed it necessary to establish another site.

The cane work of the huts was resistant to termites and if it was not plastered, it could also provide ventilation for the hut. This type of hut construction was particularly attributed to the Metu and it was unknown among their neighbours.

It is said that previously, skilled builders from Metu would be commissioned by the *Laropi* to build them huts at a price of five goats or a bull. In addition, they would drink as much beer as they wanted.

## Economy

Traditionally, the Metu were traders. They did not have to cultivate because the commerce and industry which they practised sufficed for their subsistence needs. Commerce was natural to them and through trade, they obtained food.

Besides, they also engaged in iron-working. All the deposits of iron ore in Madi were located in the Metu country. Most of the men amongst them were expert iron-workers. They could make hoes, spears and arrows for barter trade with their neighbours. The women could also barter *era* and *awa* (shea-butternuts) as well as grinding stones for food.

# The Okebu

The Okebu form one of the seven ethnic groups which inhabit the northwestern section of Uganda. They live between the Alur, the Lendu and the Lugbara on the high grasslands in the extreme northwest of Uganda.

## Origins

Okebu traditions insist that they are of Sudanic origin and they were the second to migrate from the north and to cross the Nile following the Lendu and, they in turn, were followed by the Madi.

They inhabit and cultivate on both sides of the Uganda-Zaire border in the region between Logiri and Kano. A quarter of their total population lives in Uganda. The Alur call them the *Okebu* but the Lugbara call them the *Ndo*. In fact part of their section which lives in Zaire is also known as the Ndo. Their language is significantly different from that of the Lugbara but some anthropologists prefer to group them with the Lugbara in the Madi-Moru group.

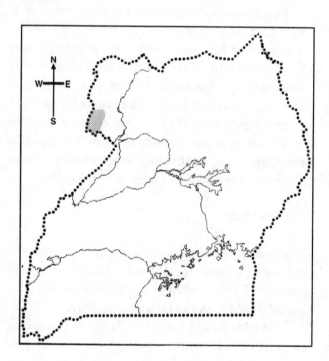

## Economy

Principally, the Okebu were mixed agriculturists. They grew a variety of crops and also kept some cows, goats and sheep. In the area of art, they had a reputation as outstanding ironworkers. During famines, they migrated to other areas and they were welcomed, protected and valued because of their skills. Even today, one can trace among the Alur, the Kakwa, the Lugbara and the Madi some iron-workers who are Okebu in origin but who might not know their Okebu connections.

## Legend

The Okebu have a legend to explain their monopoly of the art of ironworking. It says that originally, all the three – the Okebu, the Lendu and the Madi – shared the art of ironworking but the Lendu and the Madi lost their skills at a beer party.

The story goes that when all the three groups were in the middle of the smelting process, the industrious Okebu remained to finish off their work before joining the others in taking beer. This precautionary measure enabled the Okebu to avoid the accident which befell the Lendu and the Madi when their unattended-to furnace caught fire and their skin bellows destroyed while they were drinking beer.

The Okebu were very proud of their art of ironworking. Most of them doubted the ability of others, be they Lugbara or even Europeans. Their art of ironworking was however destroyed by colonialism. The colonisers insisted on importing iron implements from Europe and discouraged the traditional Okebu iron-workers. This has greatly undermined the traditional role of the Okebu smiths who are still active in the area between Arua and Godi. They make small weeding hoes, slashers and knives for sale in their local markets.

In the Zani region of Zaire, the Okebu continued to practise their craft of ironworking until 1950 when it was also outlawed by the Belgian colonial government.

# -6-
# Musical Instruments of Uganda

## Introduction

Musical instruments play an important role in Ugandan communities. They contribute to the social, psychological, therapeutical and educational existence of the people. Musical instruments constitute a large portion of people's cultural heritage and history. In day-to-day activities of people, musical instruments feature in one way or another.

Musical instruments of Uganda bear different features, belong to different classes, and serve different functions. They differ in tone, quality, timbre and resonance from one community to another depending on the value attached to the instrument. Some instruments are similar from community to community for historical reasons. They may have had the same origin or lived together for some time. This relationship is also noted in the instruments of the neighbouring countries.

An internationally accepted classification method has been used in listing these musical instruments.

## (a)  Membranophones

This class of musical instruments is composed of drums of varying sizes and shapes. Drums are made by fixing, tying or fastening animal skins on wooden frames. The skins may be thin, light or thick. The frames also differ in

*Ugandan traditional musicians at a show in West Germany*

shape. These two factors combine to produce the required quality of sound.

With the modernisation of technology some plastic and metallic materials have been introduced to serve as frames. Rubber is also being used in place of skins. This is not widespread though. The traditional standards are still dominant.

## Drums of Uganda

Drums are perhaps the most popular musical instruments in Uganda. Only small portions of Karamoja and Sebei do not use drums at all. Because of the continental predominance of drums, it is hard to trace the origins of each type of drum. The commonest method of making drums is to make a cavity in a tree-trunk after it has been cut to the size required by the drum-maker. The wood is selected from material which is not susceptible to boring insects or easy rotting. The wood is seasoned by keeping it in a place offering good conditions for a length of time to avoid it warping. When it is ready, some preservatives are applied to the wood and the skin. Some repellent herb is enclosed inside the frame in order to repel insects which could damage the skin and the wooden frame. Light and thin skins from crocodiles, monitor lizards (*African varanidae*) or alligator are used to make cylindrical long drums of a delicate type played exclusively by hand. These types of drums are covered only on one end. Pegs are used to fasten the delicate skin onto the larger shaped end of the hollowed out frame.

The relatively thick and heavy skins of cows, goats and other animals are used to make small, medium size and big drums which are played using wooden sticks or hands. These drums are usually covered on both ends. Straps hold the membranes to the required pitch.

These drums are used for a variety of purposes.

## Drums for communication

Drums offer a very effective system of communication. Different patterns of sounding a drum could summon members of a particular society to convene for hunting. The messages transmitted indicated the place of assembly, the type of hunting implements to bring and the type of animals to be hunted. However, in the modern era, not many people can discern coded messages sounded on the drums or on wind instruments. Drums were also used to warn people of danger, to declare war and to summon people to assemble. Drums are still used in some areas to get people together for communal work. The work activities range from road construction or repair to group cultivation of crops. Communal cultivation is common where a lot of un-cultivated land is available.

## Drums for rituals

Drums are used in ceremonies of installing kings, or chiefs; traditional worship, therapeutic treatment, exorcism and twin ceremonies.

In the areas of Buganda, Ankole, Bunyoro and Toro which had monarchies, the drums acquired a special status associated with royalty. Special drums were played at the birth of a royal child, at the installation of a new king and at a burial. Each occurrence and occasion had its own style and pattern of sounding drums. These drums also acquired special names which distinguished · them from ordinary types, e.g. *mujaguzo* in Buganda; *bagyendanwa* in Ankole kingdom and *mirembe* in Toro and Bunyoro.

Traditionally, drums and other special instruments for palaces were made by special people. These were experts and their offices were hereditary. They were honoured to choose someone from among themselves to stay in the palace to look after the drums for the king. This was the practice in all the king-

*Ronald Muwenda Mutebi II sounding the Majaguzo Namanyonyi royal drum at Kabowa before his coronation*

doms as well as in some chiefdoms. In some cases, only certain members of a particular clan were qualified to play the royal drums for different occasions. Otherwise, court-musicians were chosen on merit. They were required to declare their allegiance to the king.

Royal drums were beautifully decorated with coloured beads and cowrie shells of different sizes and shapes. Their royalty could be seen in the style of decoration.

In Buganda, some of the royal drums were played using decorated bones of dead people in place of wooden sticks. The bones were decorated with beads. They were especially used to announce the death of a king. The style of playing drums on anniversaries or installations of kings varied.

Another important set of drums connected with Buganda royalty is the *entenga* drums. These drums are believed to have been adopted by King Mulondo in about the 16th century and ordered by the king to be brought and played in the palace because of the beauty of the music these drums produce. A ruling was made then to have them played whenever the *Kabaka* was at home, early in the morning and late in the evening. These drums ceased to be made and played elsewhere except in the palace by people from the *Lugave* clan.

## Drums for traditional worship and healing rituals

Drums are used in traditional worship to evoke ancestral spirits to bring about desired results. In traditional worship and healing, instruments were accompanied with special songs and dances. Both drums and the music they played were classified as sacred and could not be played elsewhere or for any other purpose. These sets of drums are: *Enswezi* and *amayebe* drums of Busoga, *etida* of Teso, *bul jok* of Lango and Acholi, *Lubale* drums of Buganda. The dances also were named after those drums. They are danced to by the healers and the clients. Many of the dancers are said to get possessed by the spirits educed by the drums. Other musical instruments associated with worship and healing were gourds, rattles (*ensasi* in a number of Bantu languages). Although both drums and rattles are now used in other ways their sacred role is still respected especially when used for therapeutic purposes.

### Drums for twin ceremonies

As soon as twins are born, they are greeted with a special ululation to announce their arrival. There follows the sounding of a particular drum to confirm the news carried by the ululation.

This drum called *engalabi* and *engaabe* in Luganda and Lusoga respectively, and *emiidiri* in Ateso is long and cylindrical. Techniques of playing drums at twin ceremonies are distinctively different from those of ordinary dances. They vary from one ethnic group to another. The styles of dancing range from being close to familiar dances to completely unfamiliar styles that a stranger to the tradition would classify as total obscenity. Most parts of western Uganda do not honour the birth of twins. Thus there is no apparent musical activity associated with twins. The tradition regards the birth of twins as a curse, therefore it does not deserve any celebration.

### Drums for dances

With the exception of a small portion of Karamoja, most kinds of dance music in Uganda would be incomplete without the use of drums. Drums are responsible for differences in the dance styles. Some dances like *Bakisimba* and *Amagunju* of Buganda,

*Tamenha Ibuga* of Busoga, *Amakondere* of Bunyore and *Ekizino* of Ankole acquired royal status in those areas, while *Bwola* of Acholi and *Ajos* of Teso were popularised for the installation of chiefs.

In Acholi almost every home had at least one small drum for each *Bwola* dancer. *Bwola* dancers are co-ordinated by a big drum, *bul* during the dance.

## (b) Idiophones

This class of musical instrument is percussive. It includes those which are struck, slapped, hit, punched, knocked, rubbed, smitten or shaken, i.e. drums, logs, xylophones, maracas or shakers (*ensasi*). This class constitutes perhaps the largest collection of Ugandan musical instruments. Activities like striking parts of the body, metal, wood or stamping on the ground produce percussive effects. This testifies to the spontaneity and freedom Ugandans owe to rhythm and musical sound. As may be seen, some of these temporary musical instruments are discarded after use.

*A Muganda musician plays a rattle made from reeds and lily seeds*

# (c) Aerophones

These are the musical instruments which are blown in order to produce sound by the air vibrating. An interesting instrument in this category is human hands. Hands can be clapped in many ways to form musical instruments. Air is blown across to produce inconceivable musical sounds. Ugandans have numerous musical instruments in this class, some of which are improvised and used for an occasion and then discarded. There are a variety of wind instruments which can be categorised into two: the hard-blown and the soft-blown musical instruments.

## Hard-blown wind instruments

Hard-blown instruments are so categorised because to get sound from them requires expending a lot of energy. The *arupepe* of Teso and Karamoja made of long cow horn with only one mouth-hole, is used for communicating messages. The *amakondere* of Buganda, Bunyoro and Toro, *agwara* of West Nile and the *amagwala* of Busoga are long trumpets/horns made of wooden hollowed out frames which are larger at one end and have a hole to blow through. These instruments are played in sets. They are covered with cow-skin to give a beautiful finish of different colours. All these sets are royal instruments. In Buganda, Bunyoro and Toro they were used in palaces at ceremonies like the crowning and marriages of kings, anniversaries and burials. This tradition was carried to Busoga by the Banyoro. In West Nile the set was used for installation of their chiefs and for big occasions. While the cowhorns are played singly, the sets of the royal trumpets are played to a melodic song. They can be accompanied with a set of drums or played singly.

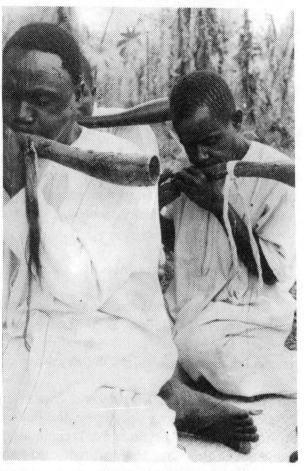

*Playing Amakondere*

## Soft-blown instruments

This category of instruments is so named because of the ease with which the sound is produced. Unlike the hard-blown instruments, these require relatively effortless techniques. The wind is blown into the mouth-hole to cause the sound to come from the instrument itself with almost no need lip vibrations. Soft-blown instruments range from hand cavity clay types, goat horns to small horns from game animals. They all belong to the flute division of musical instruments. The *Omukuri* of Ankole and Kigezi, *endere* of Buganda, *akalere* of Busoga and *alamaru* of Teso have similar makes and uses. The instrument is blown at the slightly v-shaped slit end

*Playing Endere*

of the instrument usually with four finger side holes. In Ankole, the instrument is also played and at times accompanied by drums. When not played for dancing it provides good melodies for grazing cattle and for love songs. In Buganda it can be played solo, in two's/three's or even small ensembles. An ensemble consists of the largest flute (*kiwuwa*), second largest (*Enkoloozi*); third largest (*Entengezi*); and the smallest (*Entengo*). In Busoga it is a dominant instrument played in combination with other instruments in percussion and wind sections. The Teso flute is solo or accompanies an *akogo* set. The soft-blown instruments tend to be highly localised. Some are used as children's toys. They are used and then discarded.

## (d) Chordophones

"Chord" literally means a string. It can be made from spinning or twisting sisal, skin-strips or fibre-tissues. Instruments which have these strings fastened in different ways to different shapes of frames are picked, plucked,

strummed, hit or struck. Uganda has many different instruments falling in this category. Some of them are so temporary that they are not mentioned in the list. A typical example of these is a string held on one end by biting with the teeth and pulled on the other by the left hand while the right hand plucks it or gives finger strokes to it. Different notes are arrived at by releasing and tensing the string accordingly. When the player is satisfied, the string is thrown away and forgotten.

String instruments can be categorised into two sections: the single string and multiple string. String musical instruments are as widespread in Uganda as the drums. There are incomparably more drum players than there are string instrument players.

### Single-string musical instruments

The tube fiddle is variously called *endingire, akadingidi, endingidi, esiriri or shilili* in a number of Bantu languages and *arigirigi, rigirigi* by non-Bantu speakers. It takes its name from the bowing action and the kind of sound the instrument produces. It is interesting how all sections took the imitation of the sound of the instrument to be the name of the instrument. In all languages this instrument is played to enunciate words and phrases as if to parrot human language. It is essentially a solo instrument with voice but can also be played as a duet, a trio or together with other instruments.

There are also less popular one-string instruments like *sekutulege* or *aunene* (ground bow) in Buganda and Teso respectively.

### Multiple-string instruments

These are different in shape. The eight-stringed *ennanga* of Buganda and the six-stringed *adeudeu* of Teso (bow-harp) are similar in shape with the eight or more stringed *adungu* of West Nile.

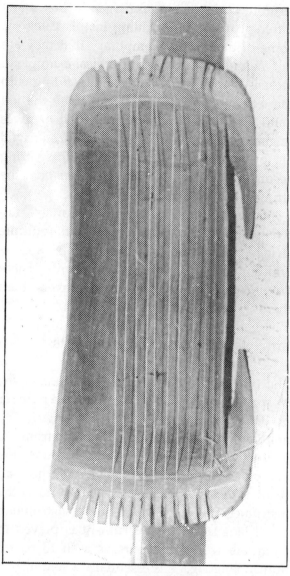

*Enanga from Ankole*

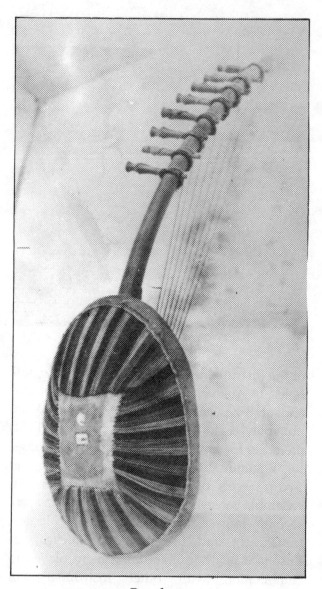

*Bow harp*

It is so named because it consists of a curved stick that is attached to a trough which is covered with a skin. The lower end of the stick is fixed to the further end of the trough. Strings attached to this part of the stick are passed through the skin and are tied to pegs driven into holes drilled at almost equal intervals in the upper part of the stick. The picture of a bow harp is shown above.

In the class of lyres comes the famous *entongoli* of Buganda sometimes called *endongo* when played to lead a wedding dance, *embaga*.

In eastern Uganda a similar instrument called *litungu* of Bagisu provides music for the shoulder dance commonly called *kamabega*. In the class of zithers comes the *nnanga* of Kigezi and Acholi.

String instruments emphasise the narrative and story-telling traditions of the people of Uganda. Love songs, songs of praise, epics, dirges, and joyous messages are some of the typical styles covered by musicians engaged in playing string instruments.

# -7-
# Traditional Crafts of Uganda

Art and craft are part of our culture. Crafts have been developed through the traditions of the people. Art and craft are a result of the feelings of the people responding to a variety of historical events and influences and to the environment in a most spontaneous manner. Art is the creation of works of beauty through the application of skill resulting from knowledge and regular practice. Craft on the other hand is taken as an occupation, especially one in which skills or techniques in the use of the hands are needed.

Craftsmanship in Uganda is a practice that has been passed down from generation to generation. It includes crafts like basketry, pottery, wood-curving and the like.

Ugandan craft works are so varied that one needs to pay attention to the various ethnic settings in order to exhaust it . One has also to make distinctions and give similarities that occur within the crafts of different ethnic groups. The differences that appear in crafts are consequences of the cultural practices of each ethnic group.

Further still, ethnologists hold that since multi-headed spears are almost always connected with ceremonial or magico-religious practices, so are the multi-mouthed pots. In Buganda the multi-mouthed pots were used to give poisoned beer to the victim who had incurred the wrath of Kabaka. The Luo and some Bantu groups – the Basamia and Bagwe – use a double-mouthed pot in certain religious rites, especially those connected with the birth of twins.

Generally, on the domestic and cultural level Ugandan crafts can be identified under the following categories: gourd vessels and wood vessels for food and drinks; pottery; pipes; basketry; stools; miscellaneous household objects; clothing and adornments; skins and barkcloth; tails and aprons; belts and girdles; hair dressing; headdresses and facial ornaments; neck, arm, and leg ornaments; shields, spears, bows and arrows; swords; dancing weapons; hunting knives; finger knives and wrist knives; hunting gear; and sound instruments.

*Graphite pots from Bunyoro*

Although there are differences that are prominent, especially as regards their functions and designs, there are qualities that bind crafts together. In this respect one should look at the very methods by which different craft-works are made by different nationalities. For example, the large field and storage baskets used in Teso are made using wicker-work with heavy materials. Wicker-work baskets are also common among the Basoga, Banyoro, Bahutu and Acholi.

The local potter in the village builds his pots of whatever description and function from the base upwards to the rim. The potter uses the coiling method. Thus the method of pottery making is the same for the Alur, the Batooro, the Basoga, and the Lango. Generally, pottery is the work of the specialised craftsman. Among some ethnic groups like the Langi, Bakiga, and the Bahutu, however, the men make the pots for their households. In most tribes the potter is an insignificant member of the community, while among the Baganda, the royal potters who worked for the Kabaka had a special title, special privileges like exemption from the *lumalo* tax and wore special aprons as their insignia. Among the Bavuma the industry entails considerable

*Ankole milk pots*

co-operation between a number of people of both sexes; women make pots while men act as middlemen and salesmen. In the case of Baganda, Banyoro and Basoga the potters are men and there are strong taboos against women approaching the clay pits. For Bavuma, Bagisu, Acholi and Madi, the potters are women. Yet in other tribes both men and women do pottery. These include the Bakiga, Bahutu, and Bairu. While the process of pot building is very similar in every tribe, there are still variations in the time taken drying and the method of firing.

Making musical instruments involves men. Even the use and manipulation of musical instruments such as drums and fiddles was strictly meant for men alone. However, due to external influence and the introduction of schools today, all sorts of people participate fully in the playing of musical instruments.

Basketry is one of the most highly developed crafts in Uganda. It is at the foundation of home making. Basketry is essential in building houses, stockades, fences or enclosures, pens, traps for wild animals, baskets and mats. Recently redesigning has been emphasised to produce modern items like handbags, table mats, flat trays, ornamental baskets and mats with different patterns. Most of these come from Buganda, Toro, Kigezi and Bunyoro.

Barkcloth-making and related crafts are also common mostly in the Bantu regions. The cloth is obtained from the bark of *Ficus natalansis* tree (*omutuba*). The process involves the use of a specially made heavy, grooved mallet (*ensaamu*). As the craftsman hits the bark with the mallet, the fibrous bark becomes thinner and larger. Traditionally, the barkcloth was purposely made to be used as burial shrouds, bedding and clothing; and carpeting the floor of the kings' palaces, especially in Buganda, Toro and Bunyoro. As the barkcloth was replaced by cotton and other clothing materials, new items like table mats, shoulder bags, hand bags, briefcases, purses, cushion covers and others have been made from barkcloth.

In most cultures, the making of metallic tools and other utilities by blacksmiths was also a common practice. Blacksmiths made cutting tools, the majority of which were the spears and arrows.

Wood-carving is also another sector which has thrived traditionally and still thrives today in Uganda. However, it has been very much influenced by external forces, especially in terms of designs.

The commonest domestic woodcraft products include: stools, beds, mortars and pestles, bowls, ladles, trays, wooden canoes and others. Some carvings are also done as decorations taking the form of masks, *omweso* boards, walking sticks and others.

Traditional craft items in Ugandan cultures include amulets, necklaces or beads, arm and leg ornaments, bracelets, rings, and headdresses. For example, the Karimojong headdress is made from human hair felted together with grease and clay. It is strengthened by a wire framework round the front edge. It is patterned with red, blue and yellow paint. The metal eyelets across the crown and at the back are used to hold ostrich feathers and other ornaments.

Witchcraft also exists in all nationalities. Objects vary according to the powers possessed by the user. Some may include decorated leopard skins, cow tails, animal horns, skins of snakes, feathers of rare birds, shells and beads.

In modern times, there are clashes between cultures. In Buganda for example, there are immigrants from all parts of Uganda and beyond. There is thus a country-wide tendency of cultures influencing one another as regards crafts and art. This, however, could lead to a strong political, social and economic integration in the sense that ethnocentricism could die at a fast rate.

*Above : Nubian baskets.   Below : Water pots from Busoga*

There has also been a profusion of new materials and techniques. Plastic and aluminium products, for instance, have caused the dwindling of utilitarian local crafts like pottery. More and more people in Uganda are using plastic ware like jerrycans, mugs and bowls. Most Ugandan crafts have therefore become ornamental.

This has brought Ugandan craftsmen together with one common need: to sell their work. In the past when the markets were local, when life moved at a slow and even tempo and there were no buyers from overseas, there was no need to redesign the traditional craft for modern use. While the production of craftworks by local craftsmen for sale is fairly recent, it is fast-growing and has great potential. The main ideas behind it have been to preserve and encourage indigenous methods, to create jobs for local people, especially women, and to exploit the huge foreign market.

# -8-
# Education and Cultural Transformation

Although their cultures differed greatly in most aspects, the pre-colonial Ugandan societies shared a common education system. Prior to the coming of the Christian missionaries, there existed no schools of the type that we have today. Nonetheless, people were educated and trained. There existed what the Europeans described as informal education. There were no defined institutions of learning, no particular teachers, no blackboards or pencils and books, but children could be taught all the same. In all the societies, the system of instruction tended to be similar; only the subject matter or syllabus differed according to the particular needs and social values of the given society.

The traditional education system was designed to create an ideal individual who could fully fit into and be accepted by society. Accordingly, discipline and respect were emphasised. The instruction normally took place round the fireplace after the evening meal or whenever a child committed an offence. Through stories, tales and riddles, the mother or grandmother would alert the children to what society expected of them as they grew up. The fathers would, through proverbs, stories and direct instruction, teach the young boys their expected roles in society. Some societies used capital punishment to alert the young generations to the gravity of particular cases of indiscipline and immorality. The Bakiga, for instance, would end the life of a pregnant girl by tying and throwing her down a steep cliff in order to teach those who contemplated having sex before marriage that

the consequences were bitter. As for the Banyankore, they would curse and disown the girl who became pregnant for reasons similar to those of the Bakiga. The Langi and the Acholi would fine the boy heavily for such misconduct. This would help to persuade the young that such an act was socially undesirable.

If, for example, a man was caught committing adultery with another man's wife among the Kakwa, the Alur, the Lugbara, the Langi, the Iteso and the Acholi he would be killed by the offended party and there would be no case to answer. Among the Karimojong, the offended man would confiscate all the cattle of the offender and he would continue to confiscate everything the offender would come to possess until such a time as sufficient honour had been restored to the offended. Some other punitive measures were taken to curb indiscipline and dishonesty in society. The punishments varied according to the weight of the offence as it was viewed by a given society. Most societies decried stealing and sorcery and in an attempt to educate the young not to indulge in such activities, the thieves and the sorcerers were either chased away from the village or even killed.

Education was not only confined to discipline. It was an all-round process which catered for all facets of the individual. Apart from morals, it also catered for the mind and the hand. There was nothing like irrelevant education. All that was taught was geared towards the creation of an ideal individual who would ably fit into the society in which he was born and lived. In order to encourage togetherness and co-operation, the history of the society was often recounted. Among the Kakwa, the Baganda and the Banyoro, there were special persons entrusted with the duty of recounting the history of those societies. The people were taught about their origins, their relations with their neighbours as well as the common instances of rejoicing and suffering. The main purpose in this recounting of the peoples' historical and social traditions was to enable the society to retain a common heritage and identity.

It was imperative that the young be taught their cultural values, norms, taboos and totems. The young were taught the do's and don'ts of the society into which they were born. They were taught about their clans and the totems and taboos of those clans. Besides, they were also taught about their clan relations and their boundaries in order to avoid incest. The boys were taught and trained to grow up into responsible men in much the same way as the girls were groomed to grow up into responsible housewives. The boys among the Bakonjo, Bamba, Bagisu and also girls among the Sabiny were initiated into manhood and womanhood by undergoing the ritual of circumcision. Accordingly, the fathers would train the boys in methods of herding, fighting, hunting, agriculture and trade. And the mothers would instruct the young girls in the proper ways of cooking, basketry, pottery, childcare, dressing and other functions related to housekeeping.

As for the technical skills, there was what is generally referred to as learning-by-doing. Boys would acquire skills while working alongside their fathers just as the girls would duly acquire skills by working alongside their mothers. If one's father was a blacksmith, his son would learn the art by working with him. This helps to explain why some skills like ironworking, rainmaking, divination, healing,

pottery and several other specialties tended to be hereditary. As a result, one finds that the Okebu were renowned iron-workers, the Banabuddu of Buganda were barkcloth makers, the Banyoro were good potters and makers of red-hoes, the Banyakore were good red-spear makers (*emitari*) etc. These skills were not found generally within each society but they were particular to individual clans within the given society.

In general terms, therefore, if one wants a striking example of education for decent living, pre-colonial Uganda provided it. Those who mastered the skills in their respective fields were held in high esteem. The diviner and healer in Bugisu occupied high places. The *Etogo* or *Ateker* was as much a legislative body as the parliament of today. An expert fighter or dancer was well qualified.

The whole system of educating and training the young generations in the Ugandan societies was discouraged by colonialism. The Christian missionaries who arrived in Uganda in 1877 (the CMS), 1879 (the White Fathers), 1896 (the Mill Hill Fathers) and 1910 (the Verona Fathers) started conducting formal education. They were joined in their efforts by the colonial government after 1920. With the arrival of missionaries and the establishment of mission schools, the education system changed. Emphasis was first placed on the 3R's (writing, reading and religion). Later, the emphasis shifted to liberal arts. At present it is on sciences, at least in theory.

## Cultural Transformation

With the advent of foreign religions and colonialism in the second half of the 19th and early part of the 20th century, the traditional cultural set-up of different Ugandan societies was transformed. The whole outcome was a quasi-colonial culture which tended to describe everything African as "black" causing

*A traditional Acholi girl*

*Participants in a modern beauty contest*

the people to discard their cultural values and imitate Europeans in manners of worship, marriage, eating, walking, dressing and even talking.

The first Arab caravan trader reached Buganda in the 1840's. He was called Ahmed Bin Ibrahim. Although he was much more interested in trade than anything else, he also talked about Allah. By 1869, Kabaka Mutesa I of Buganda had already joined the other faithful in the Middle East and other parts of the Muslim world to observe the month of

Ramadan. By 1876, Islam had taken a firm root in Buganda. The other two religions of the Christian faith followed in 1877 and 1879 and by 1894, Uganda was declared a British Protectorate. Henceforth, colonialism and religion worked hand in hand to transform the various societies of Uganda into the state they are in today.

Religion and education brought about change. Prior to the intrusion of foreign religions, Ugandan societies had their own ideas of God. When the Muslims and later the

Christians came in, they described the African ideas of God as being erroneous and evil. Accordingly, they started searching around for traditional names to represent their God. The Muslims had little difficulty in getting a name. Their God was Allah and Allah he would remain. The Christians, however, needed an interpretation. In most cases, despite their misgivings, they ended up using the traditional equivalents to describe their big God. One funny instance was among the Acholi, Langi, Alur and Lugbara. Their traditional idea of God was *Jok* but the Europeans associated Jok with evil and so they forced the people to use *Lubanga* for God while Lubanga in Lwo language meant an evil spirit.

With the introduction of Islam and Christianity, it became fashionable to communicate with God in Arabic, Latin and English. The mode of worship changed greatly as the traditional shrines of the *abila* type were replaced with mosques and churches with seats, church organs and electricity. Prayers became regular on every Friday for Muslims; and Sunday for Christians or in the evenings. Praying no longer depended on particular instances of want or trouble.

Gradually religion did not only become a belief but also a way of life. Accordingly, the eating habits and manners of dress came to be styled according to religion. The Muslims took up the Arab style of dressing while the Chris-

*Kabaka Mwanga in 19th-century robes*

*His son, Kabaka Chwa, in 20th century western style military attire*

*Kizinga war fetish of Buganda, worshipped by Buganda army commanders before going to war. Such practices have been marginalised as more Ugandans turn to Christianity as demonstrated by the warm reception given to the head of the Catholic Church, Pope John Paul II on his visit to Uganda, 1993*

tians took up the European style. The African values were severely undermined by the new foreign religions and European colonialism to the extent that those who became greatly engrossed in religion and education came to despise the traditional ways of life.

The foods and eating habits have also changed. The Muslims would prefer rice and they do not eat pork and unhallowed meat. Some Christians would neither eat pork nor drink alcohol because the Israelites upon whom the Holy Bible is based were told not to do so by God. It is now fashionable for families to eat at table with forks, knives and spoons rather than sitting down. Middle-class families will be seen taking mid-morning tea with bread, butter and jam. The national days of rejoicing have been changed and the modern disc and tape recordings take precedence over the traditional songs and dances.

The traditional cultural set-up has been transformed so much that some people seem to wish themselves changed to look white or yellow. The women have been    the most

*Pope John Paul II in Fort Portal, 1993*

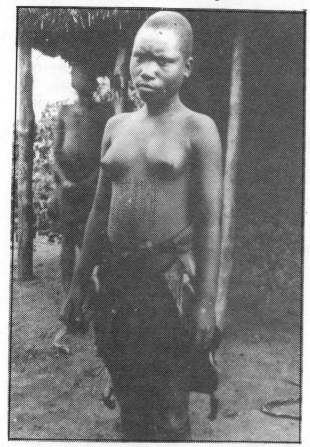

*Past and present: Karimojong girl in traditional attire and a modern Ugandan woman in a* gomesi

affected in this respect. In fact, some women would like to have their bodies resemble those of the Europeans and they would rather curl their hair or have it otherwise treated since wigs have become unfashionable.

Although generally speaking there has been a high degree of cultural transformation, some of the Ugandan societies have retained significant elements of their culture. Thus, though most people have adopted what they call the modern culture, their traditions and cultural traits can still be traced.

For example, the modern dress of the Baganda which could be said to be traditional, is the *kanzu* for the men and the *busuuti* or *gomesi* for the women. For the Banyankore, it is also the *gomesi* for the women while the men would not mind a suit in the form of a pair of trousers, a shirt, a coat and preferably also a hat. The Bakiga men prefer to dress like the Banyankore in the manner described

previously. Their women seem comfortable in the *kiteteya* with a small *suuka* flung over the shoulders. These changes have not been confined to the particular societies mentioned above but they have extended with slight variations to cover all the other societies of Uganda. In fact, due to religious influences, most people in Uganda have an Arab or European name besides their own traditional name.

In terms of political set-up, Uganda is now a republic. Her economy is partly integrated into the world capitalist system. It produces coffee, cotton, tobacco, tea, maize, rice and groundnuts for sale to other countries. In the rural areas, the traditional foods are still cultivated but in addition, cash crops are also grown. To say the least, the traditional system has been greatly transformed. In most of the Ugandan societies a new culture has replaced the traditional culture.

# Bibliography

Much of the information contained in this book was obtained from field research among the societies concerned or from members of the said societies who were living in and around Kampala, more especially at Makerere University. However, a significant portion of the information on particular aspects of some societies was obtained from the various volumes of *The Uganda Journal*. Some other information was obtained from books. Information on the religious rituals of the Alur was got from Ng'omlokojo but a significant amount of it was from Southhall. The most important sources of literature have been listed for those who may require more information about some aspects of particular societies which were, obviously, not covered in detail.

## ARTICLES IN *THE UGANDA JOURNAL* SERIES

Oliver Roland ,"Ancient Capital Sites of Ankole," UJ, 23, 1 (1959).
Oliver Roland ,"The Royal Tombs of Buganda," UJ, 23, 2 ( 1959).
Oliver Roland ,"The Baganda and the Bakonjo," UJ, 23, (1959).
Oliver Roland , "The Traditional Histories of Ankole, Buganda and Bunyoro," UJ, (1958).
Morris H. F ., "The Making of Ankole," UJ, 21,1 (1957).
Beattie J. M .H., "Nyoro Personal Names ," UJ, 21, 1 (1957).
Beattie J. M. H., "Nyoro Mortuary Rites ," UJ, 25, 2 (1961).
X. Y. Z., "Native Music," UJ, 1, 1 (1934).
Thomas, "The Inheritance of Land in Buganda," UJ, 21, 2 (1957).
Ingham , K., "Some Aspects of the History of Western Uganda,"UJ, 21, 3 (1957).
Haddow , A. J., "Whistled Signals Among the Bakonjo," UJ, 16, 2 (1952).
Crazzolara , J. P., "The Hamites : Who were they ?" UJ, 33, part 1 (1969).
White , R . G.," The Blacksmiths of Kigezi ," UJ, 33, 1 (1969).
Atanda, J. A.," The Bakopi in the History of Buganda," UJ, 33, 2 (1969).
Nabwiso-Bulima," The Evolution of the Kyabazingaship in Busoga," UJ, 33, 2 (1969).
Posnansky, M., " Bantu Genesis," UJ, 25, 1 (1961).
Ukyns William, "Blood Brotherhood in Ankole," UJ, 2, 1 (1934)
Perryman, P. W., " Native Witchcraft,"UJ, 4 (1936).
Davies , A . K.," A Glimpse on Uganda's Past," UJ, 2, 1 (1934).
A .D. F. T .," Basoga Death and Burial Rites," UJ, 2, 1 (1934).
Thomas , A . S.," Bwamba Initiation Ceremonies,"( some photographs of initiates ),UJ, 4 (1936).
A .V. O., "The Hima Method of Counting," UJ, 4 (1936).
Ukyns William, " Metamorphosis : Muzwaga's," UJ, 4 (1936).
Perry, M .R., " The Naming of Twins," UJ, 4, 2 (1936).
Bansisa, Y., "Music in Africa," UJ, 4, 2 (1936).
Peason Pete, "The Black Forest Pygmies," UJ, 4, 2 (1936).
Keens , R . S.," Reminiscences of Busoga and its Chiefs,"UJ, 4, 3 (1937).
Switzer , C. W., "The Story of Rwabinumi," UJ, 4, 3 (1937).
Perkins Temple, "Bwamba Initiation Ceremony," UJ, 4, 3 (1937).
Snoxhall, R. A. , " Coronation Rituals and Customs of Buganda," UJ, 4, 4 (1937).
K . W., "The Procedure in accession to the throne of a nominated King in the
        Kingdom of Kitara," UJ, 4, 4 (1937).
Lukyn Williams, "The Inauguration of Omugabe of Ankole to Office," UJ, 4, 4 (1937).
Lukyn Williams, "The Coronation of the Abakama of Koki," UJ, 4, 4 (1937).
Nsimbi , M . B. , " The Clan System in Buganda," UJ, 28, 1 (1964).
Bamunoba , Y. K., " Blood Brotherhood in Ankole," UJ, 28, 1 (1964).
Kaggwa , L. B.,"Lubaale Initiation in Buganda ," UJ, 28, 1 (1964).
Morris , F. M., " The Heroic Recitations of the Bahima of Ankole,"UJ, 28, 1 (1964).
K . W," Abakama of Kitara," UJ, 5, 2 (1937).
Shillit , J. F., " Etuku : A Problem Expanded ," UJ, 26, 2 (1962).
Weatherby , J. M., "A Preliminary Note on the Structure of Clan and Bororiet Among the
        Southern Groups of the Sebei Speaking Peoples," UJ, 12, 1 (1948).
Sempebwa, " Buganda Folk Songs : A Rough Classification ," UJ, 12, 1 (1948).
Wallace , J. M.," Fire Making by Friction ," UJ, 12, 1 (1948).
Jacobs, L. Benet, " A Note from Luuka County , Busoga," UJ, 13, 1 (1949).

White , R & Nkurunziza , J., " Some Petroglyphs and Petromyths in Ankole and, Kigezi,"
          UJ, 35,  2 (1971).

Murray, " Cattle and Education  in Ankole : Status Conflict," UJ, 34,  1 (1970).

Charsley , S . R., " Mobility and  Village Composition  in  Bunyoro," UJ, 34, part 1 (1970).

Mushanga , M. T., " The Clan System Among the Banyankore," UJ, 34, part 1 (1970).

Mateke , P.,  " The  Struggle for  Dominance  in Bufumbira," UJ, 34; part 1 (1970).

Mc Master , D. N., " The  Distribution of Traditional Types of Food Containers in Uganda,"
          UJ, 26, 2 (1962).

Welbourn , F. B., " Some Aspects of Kiganda  Religion," UJ, 26,  2 (1962).

Weatherby , J. M., " Interwarfare on  Mt. Elgon in the 19th and 20th Centuries,"
          UJ, 26 , 2 (1962).

Southhall, " Laws  and  Marriage  in  Uganda," UJ, 26,  2 (1962).

Nye , G. W.,  " A Legend of  Some Hills  in Bulemezi," UJ, 6, 3 (1940).

Nye , G. W., " A note on Kikasa in Bulemezi," UJ, 6,  3 (1940).

Trowell , M., " Some  Royal Craftsmen of  Buganda," UJ, 8,  2 (1941).

Posnansky , M., " Kingship, Archaeology and Historical myth," UJ, 30, 1 (1966).

Okot P'Bitek, " The Concept of Jok Among the Acholi and Lango,"UJ, 27, 1 (1963).

Thomas Loan, " The  Flat  Roofed  Homes of the Sebei at Benet," UJ,V 27, 1 (1963).

Lanning," Barkcloth  Hammers," UJ, 23, 1 (1959).

Crazzolara, " Luo  Traditions," UJ, 23, 1 (1959).

Oliver , C. D., "  Stone  Implements  in Lugbara," UJ, 23,  2 (1959).

Akena , N, " Lango  Religion," UJ, 23,  2 (1959).

Docherty , A. J., " The  Karimajong and the Suk,"UJ, 21,  1 (1957).

Bere , R . M., " Acholi  Dances," UJ, 1, 1 (1934).

Bere , R . M., " A Note  on the Origins of the Payera  Acholi," UJ, 1, 1 (1934).

Persse , E. M, " Ethnological Notes on the Karimajong," UJ, 1,  2 (1934).

Bere , R . M., " Acholi  Hunts," UJ,1, 2,1934.

Gray John, Sir, " Acholi  History ; 1860 - 1901," UJ, 16,  1 (1952).

Clark Boris, " Memorial  Service  for an  Ox in Karamoja," UJ, 16, 1 (1952).

Gulliver , P. H., " Bell  Oxen and  Ox  Names  Among  the  Jie," UJ,16, 1 (1952).

Wright , A. C . A., " Luo  Migrations : A Review, " UJ, 16,  1 (1952).

Ludger , K., "Control of Crime in Primitive Society : An Example from Teso," UJ, 16, 2 (1952).

Watson , J . M., " Agoro  Systems of Irrigation," UJ, 16,  2 (1952).

Mill Hill Fathers, "Derivations from Teso Place  Names,"UJ, 16,  2 (1952).

Poswett , " West Nile Hills and History,"  UJ, 15, (1951).

Morris , T. D. H., " Bakonjo  Shrines," UJ, 17, 1 (1953).

Lanning , E. C., " Ancient  Earthworks  in  Western Uganda," UJ, 17,  1 (1953).

Watson , J. M.,"Karimojong  Wedding," UJ, 16, 2 (1952).

          " Tribal  Nicknames : Correspondence," UJ, 16,  2 (1952).

Clerk , L., "Group  Stone  Axe : Loitome, Karamoja," UJ, 30,  2 (1966).

Higgins , S.," Acholi  Birth  Customs," UJ, 30,  2 (1966).


Berber , P . J.," Karamoja  in  1910," UJ, 28, 1 (1964).

Crazzolara," The  Luo People," UJ, 5,  1 (1937).

Birth , J. P., " Madi  Blacksmiths," UJ, 5,  1 (1937).

Birth , J. P.," Some Notes on the Metu People of West  Madi," UJ, 5, .2 (1937).

Malandra , Rev.Fr," The  Ancestral  Shrine of the  Acholi," UJ, 6,  1 (1939).

Lukyn Williams," Teso  Clans," UJ, 4,  2 (1936).

Olyechi Erimayo, "The Anointing of Clan Heads Among  the  Lango," UJ, 4, 4, (1937).

Ogot B. A.," Traditional Religion and the Precolonial History of Africa : The Example of the
          Padhola," UJ, 31,  part 1 (1967).

Sharman & Anderson, "Drums of the Padhola," UJ, 31,  2 (1967).

Robinns , L.,"Rock Paintings at Napedul Hill," UJ, 34,  part 1 (1970).

Morton , W. H.," Rock  Engravings  from Loteteleit, Karamoja," UJ, 31,  2 (1967).

Wilson J . H., " Preliminary observation  of the Oporom People of Karamoja, their Ethnic
          Status, Culture and Postulated  Relation  to the Peoples of the late Stone Age,"
          UJ, 34,  part 2 (1970).